Carving Scandinavian Santas

Ken Blomquist

Text written with and photography by ***Jeffrey B. Snyder***

Schiffer Publishing Ltd®

4880 Lower Valley Road, Atglen, PA 19310 USA

Contents

Old Swedish postcard, c. 1915.

Library of Congress Control Number: 2004108536

Designed by Mark David Bowyer
Type set in Bodoni Bd BT/Humanist 521 BT

ISBN: 0-7643-2133-1
Printed in China

Published by Schiffer Publishing Ltd.
4880 Lower Valley Road
Atglen, PA 19310
Phone: (610) 593-1777; Fax: (610) 593-2002
E-mail: Info@schifferbooks.com

In Europe, Schiffer books are distributed by
Bushwood Books
6 Marksbury Ave.
Kew Gardens
Surrey TW9 4JF England
Phone: 44 (0) 20 8392-8585; Fax: 44 (0) 20 8392-9876
E-mail: info@bushwoodbooks.co.uk
Free postage in the U.K., Europe; air mail at cost.

Acknowledgments

There are some very special people that I must thank for making this book possible. John and Jeanne Fitzpatrick encouraged me to carve an authentic Swedish Santa. Natalie Jordan used her artistic skill to turn my ideas into a workable pattern. Dennis Kennedy, John Thomas, and Mike Coldren supplied material, ideas, and photographs that made the business of Santa carving a little easier. My daughter Kate's creativity always inspires me and my wife Mary makes my work possible.

As always, special thanks go to my editor, Jeff Snyder, and publishers, Peter and Nancy Schiffer, for their patience, help, and encouragement.

Old Swedish postcard, c. 1915.

Old Swedish postcard, c. 1915.

Introduction

Sweden's Jultomten

Swedish postcards featuring the Jultomten, as portrayed by the artist Jenny Nystrom (1854-1946).

I began carving my series of Santas in 1990. I create a Santa from a different country or legend each year and try to base my designs on historical documentation. When Christmas Day is over and New Year's Day approaches, I begin planning my next design. I use a variety of books for history and legends, but pictures are often hard to find. I have used the Rare Book and Ephemera collection at Winterthur Museum for much of my research.

The Fitzpatricks, who collect my Santas, had often asked me to carve a Swedish Santa. Because my paternal grandparents were born in Sweden, I have always wanted to carve a Jultomten, but had been unable to find good pictures. Last winter, I found two sets of Swedish Christmas postcards on eBay. As soon as the package arrived from Sweden, I began work on my 2003 design.

Before the nineteenth century, Swedish legend told of a goat who delivered gifts, but Jultomten joined or replaced him in the 1800s. Jultomten, who has a fondness for rice pudding, comes to the door on Christmas Eve, looking for good children (and a bowl of pudding). The postcards depict an elf-like figure carrying a basket filled with toys and wrapped parcels, sealed with wax.

The legends and traditions of Norway and Finland are quite similar to those of Sweden. In Norway the little guy is known as Julesvenn and in Finland as Tomte.

Note

Jultomten has been an exciting and very popular carving for me. He does, however, take considerable time and planning. Please read through the book and note the materials suggestions before purchasing supplies and beginning your carving.

Throughout the book, I use different carvings of Jultomten from different stock in order to illustrate both variations and diverse aspects of carving. Additionally, I must confess that, in order to complete this book in a timely fashion, it was necessary to precut and work from several blanks.

Tools and Supplies

transparent medium
- tracing vellum
- Plexiglas™
- clear acetate (presentation cover)

band saw with 1/4" skid tooth blade (4tpi)

combination square
drill press or hand drill – 1/16", 1/8", 3/8", and 1/2" drill bits
hot glue gun
carving knives
leather strop and oil
aluminum oxide
flexible shaft machine
 carbide bits
 steel cutting bits
 carving stones
dividers or calipers
cyanoacrylate glue (i.e. Super Glue™) and quick drying epoxy
wood burning pen
propane torch or kitchen mini torch
leather gloves and apron
3/4" brads
1/4" dowel rod
3/4" pine board
needle nose pliers
chisels
nylon scrubbing pad or fine brass or steel brush

Note: You do not need every tool listed to complete this project. You may also have additional tools not listed here that you prefer, such as a small carving chisel. The important thing is to always use the tools you are comfortable with. Experiment to make this carving your own.

Paints and Finishes

lacquer base sanding sealer
flat white spray paint
liquid oil base primer
latex white primer
acrylic paints in
 titanium white
 red
 blue
 green
 gold
 heavy body white
 flesh tones (dark and light)
 raw sienna
 burnt umber
 burnt sienna
 light blue
 Min Wax Early American™ oil base stain
 Krylon™ Spray suede paints in choice of Berber, Buckskin, Brittany, Forest Glenn
brushes
 1/2" wash brush
 #8 round
 liner
 stylus
 sponge

Hints and Suggestions

- If you trace your pattern on thin paper or use a photocopier, glue it to heavier stock to make it sturdier.
- When you cut out a Plexiglas pattern, use a band saw rather than a scroll saw. The heat generated by a high speed blade will melt the plastic.
- Use a permanent marker on Plexiglas.
- Use a hot glue gun to keep your profiles in line.
- If you notice cracks or checking in your stock, treat it with Super Glue.
- If you need to repair your carving, use auto body putty as a filler or gap filling glue. This putty dries very hard and fast, depending on the amount of hardener you use. If you are very careful, you can cut this material with a knife as soon as it begins to set up. You won't have much time, so pay attention.
- Start out with your stock as square as possible.
- Use a sharpening stone to round over the back of your band saw blade.
- When cutting out your project, nibble away at the corners. Take your time!
- Always use sharp tools and good quality paints and brushes.
- Once you have laid out your center lines, do not cut them off until you have finished rounding over all points of the body and legs.
- Clean out your carbide bits and sharpen your knives often.
- Wear a face mask when you are creating dust.
- Wear your safety goggles and turn on your dust collector.
- If you don't have a dust collector, set up a box fan with a furnace filter and set it to draw air away from you.
- Use a leather glove and apron when using a burning torch.
- If your base will not sit flat, hollow the bottom, leaving about a 1/4 inch rim around the edge. The slight depression in the bottom will take care of any high spots.

Carving Jultomten, the Swedish Santa

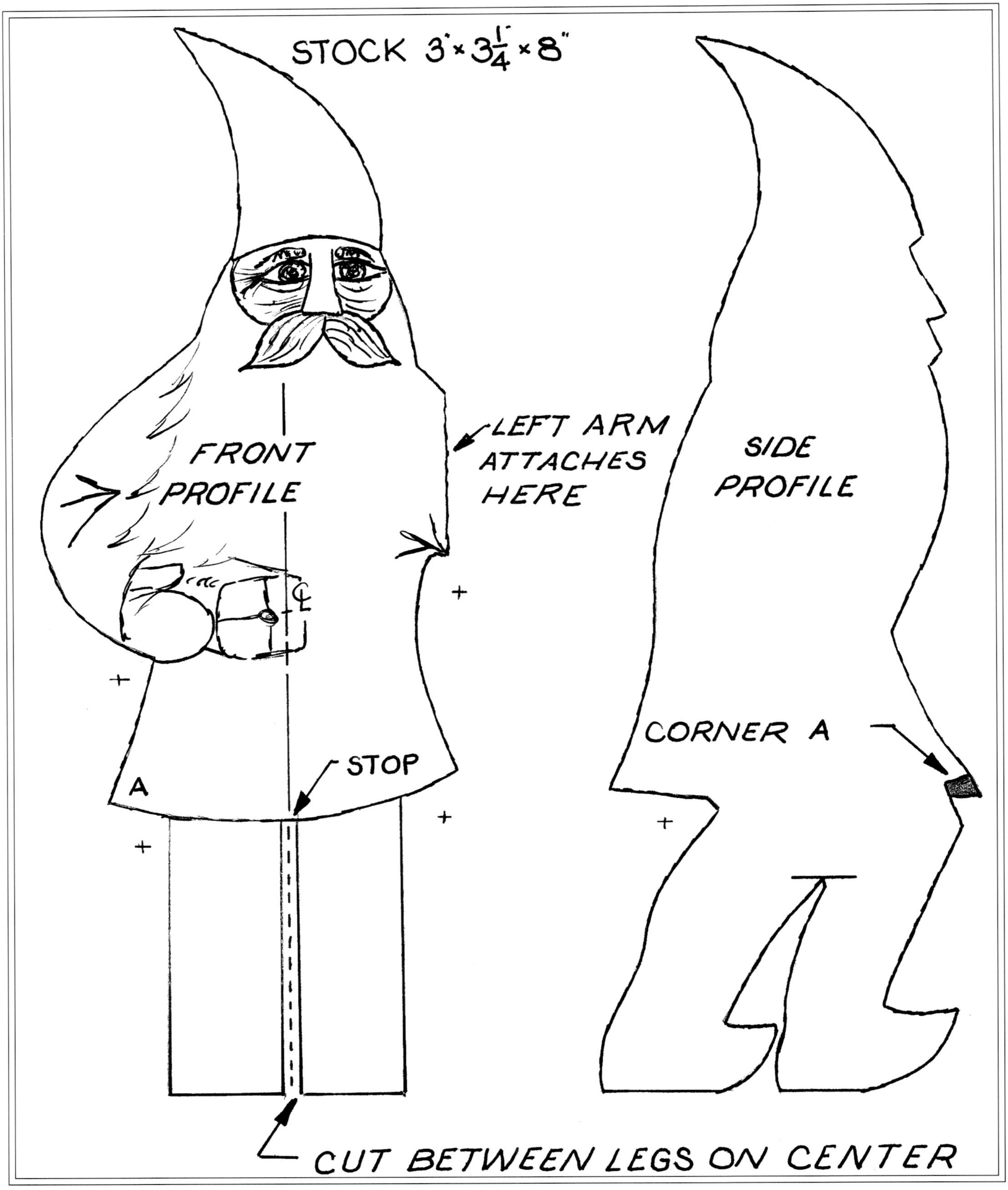

LEFT ARM - 3" × 2½" × 1¾" ROUGH STOCK

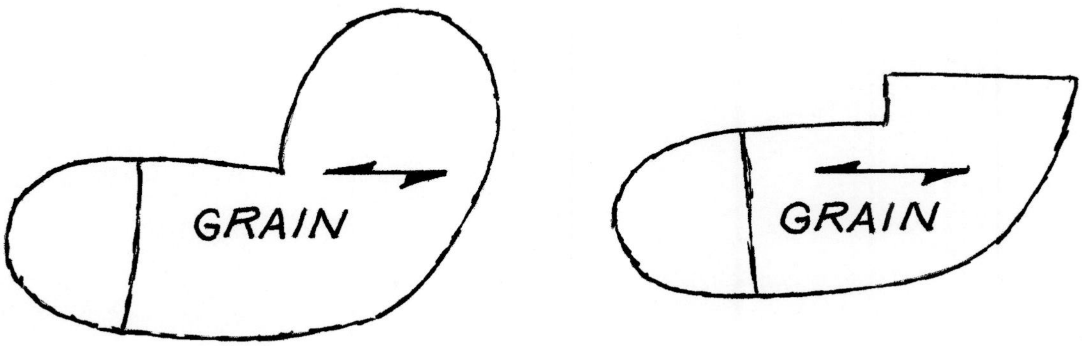

RUCKSACK 2½" × 1½" × 3"

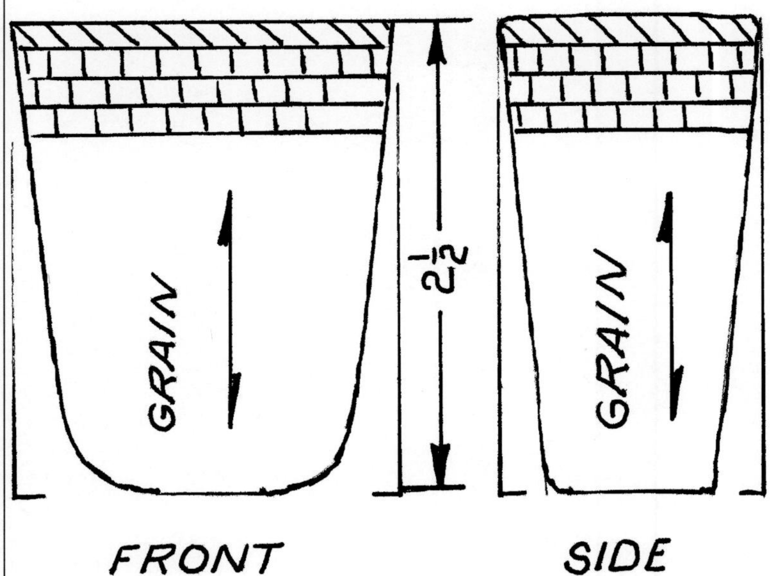

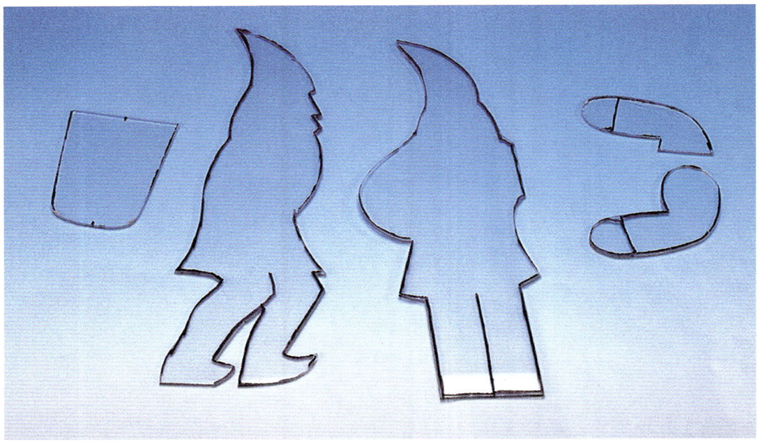

Trace the pattern onto vellum, reproduce it on a copier, or—this is a new thing for me—trace it onto Plexiglas™ with a fine point permanent marker. The advantage of Plexiglas is that you have a permanent pattern. Use a band saw to cut out the Plexiglas pattern.

Trace on the front and side profile, keeping the legs on your baseline.

In this project I will be using white cedar and white pine. The stock should be as square as possible. Using a combination square, draw a baseline for the front and side profiles, of your 3" x 3 1/4" x 8" piece of carving stock.

We want to establish lines from the bottom points of the coat.

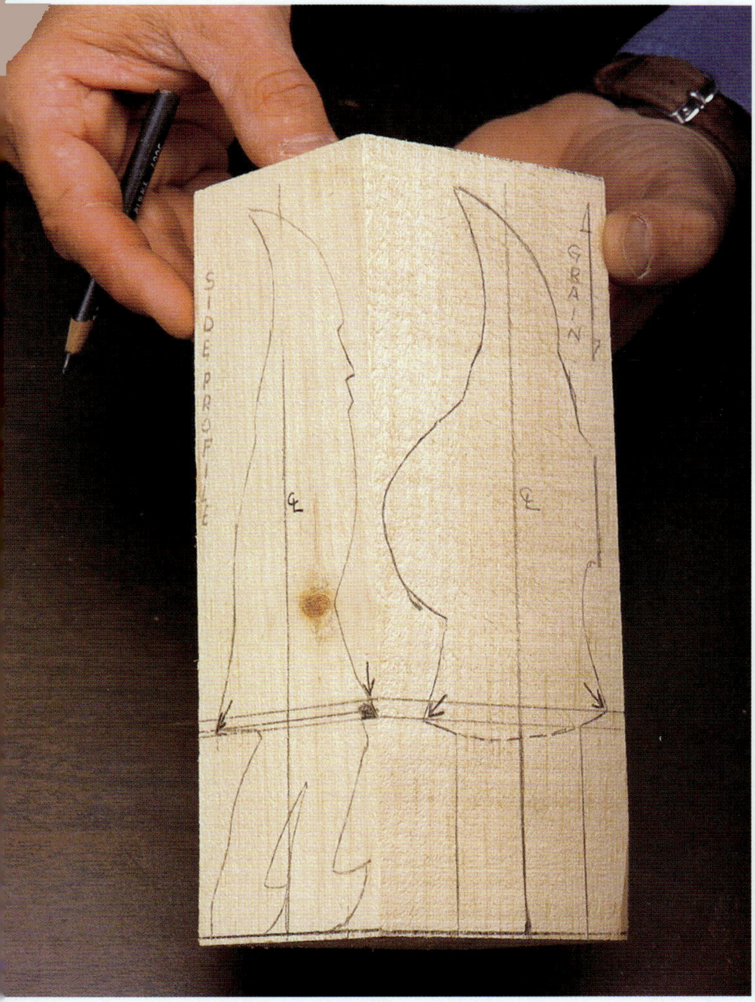

Establish centerlines on the front and side profiles. You should notice a shaded area on the side profile that needs to be added. That shaded area reflects extra coat material that is not to be removed.

I have found that drilling holes at critical points on your pattern makes cutting out your project a little easier. My suggestion is that if you have a drill press and your stock is square, drill holes at the six locations I have shown in this picture.

Using a fine sharpening stone, round over the back of your blade. My suggestion for this project is to use a 1/4" 4 tpi (teeth per inch) saw blade.

If you decide to drill with a hand drill, drill your holes as accurately and squarely as you can.

To begin the process of cutting out your project, cut on the line between the legs to the coat.

Once the front profile has been cut out, use hot glue to securely reattach the side profile pattern, gluing only on areas that will be cut away with the band saw. I've marked those areas with X's here. Make sure to apply hot glue to both top and bottom. This makes cutting out the side profile much safer and easier. Caution: do not apply too much glue, as it tends to gum up the saw blade.

While cutting the front profile, you will find it much easier to cut into the corners using the drilled holes as relief. Using the drilled holes means you will not have to back your project out of the band saw quite as often and it is easier to turn the corner.

This blade is bigger than I normally use. With a smaller blade, when cutting between the legs on the side profile, I can rotate the block around the blade to cut away excess wood down to the shoes.

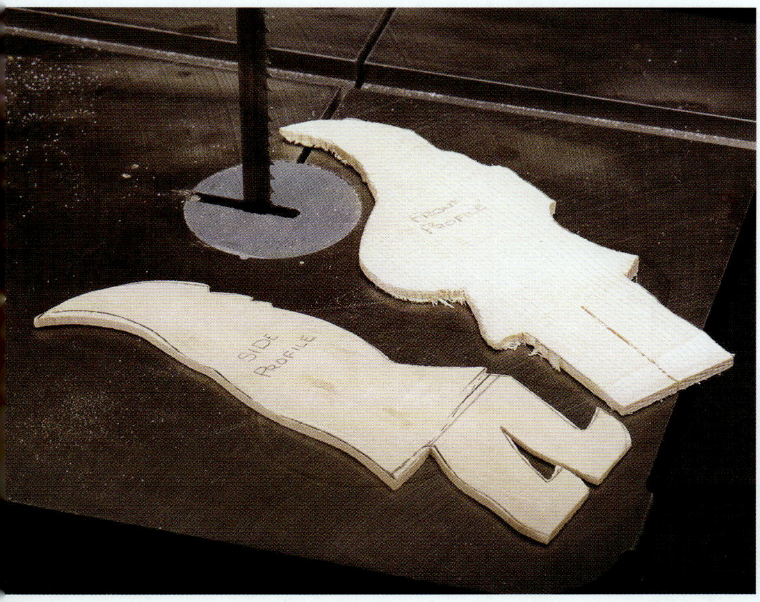

If you use a block of wood a little larger than you need for the project, you can carefully trim away the excess with the band saw, using the thin profiles created as permanent pattern templates.

Add centerlines to the right front leg and the left rear leg. Place X's on the two legs to be removed. Draw a rough oval where the missing left arm will go.

Now that your pattern is cut out, add centerlines on all four sides of the project.

The X's on the base show which legs need to be removed (do this now to avoid cutting off the wrong legs). Along the back side, we've added reference lines approximately 1/4" on either side of center on the body and 1/8" on either side of the legs. Carving to the reference lines, rather than to the centerlines, helps keep the body round.

The circle on the underside of the project represents the outline of the coat. This can be a rough circle. Remember, this is a free flowing piece of material. Don't try to achieve perfection. At this point you are ready to carve.

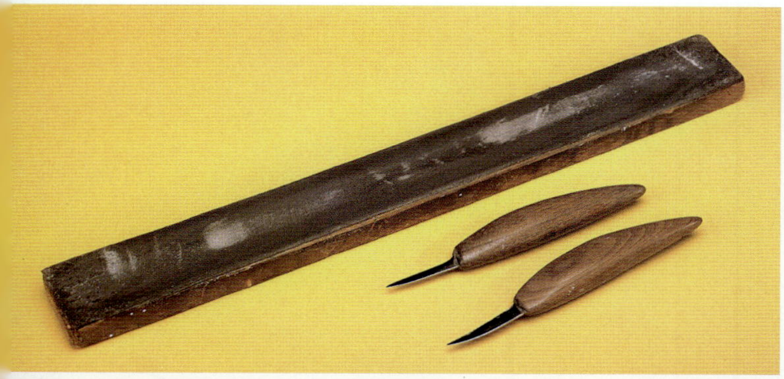

These two photos show the carving knives and sharpening strop I like to use. Before carving, always sharpen your knife by keeping the blade flat and passing it up and down the strop an equal number of times on both sides. Do this about every 20 to 30 minutes of carving time.

Start by carving away the bottom of each leg. You should start your carving at the corner of each leg. Pull the knife toward your body, using your thumb as a fulcrum, keeping your thumb on the project for safety.

To remove material from the leg, at the base of the coat, make a stop cut on the outside corner. Make it fairly deep, running parallel to the bottom edge of the coat.

Turn your knife around, carving toward the body. Cut down on the corner, toward the coat and the stop cut line. Continue cutting away excess material, carving both down toward the coat and up toward the foot.

Continue removing excess material.

Start removing material from around the bottom of the coat.

The excess has been removed; both legs are now in their proper positions.

Be sure to carve with safety in mind. I call this carving method "toward the body." Your thumb acts as an anchor. Pull the knife toward you with your thumb firmly fixed to the block of the wood but well clear of the knife blade. As long as your thumb remains on the stock, you remain in control of the knife.

You may also remove this excess wood from around the legs quickly using a Foredom™ tool with a carbide bit.

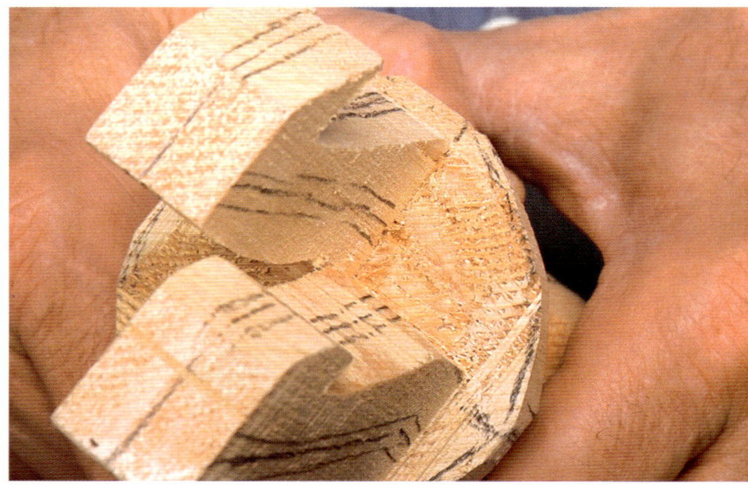

The base of the coat has been rounded.

Cut from the base of the coat up to the arms to round the coat. You will need to make a stop cut at the base of each arm to finish your cut.

Make the stop cut at the base of each arm on all four sides.

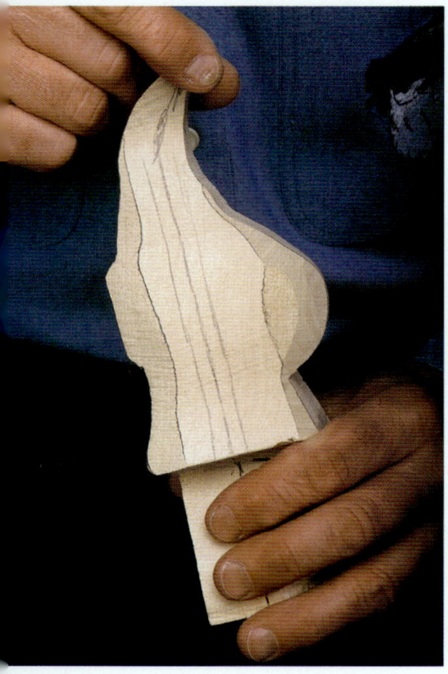

For more experienced carvers, who are more comfortable with the band saw, you can use your band saw to carve off a little more of the excess wood.

You may also use a Foredom tool instead of a knife to round off the coat. With the Foredom tool it is a little easier to create flair at the base of the coat. The knife tends to flatten the edge.

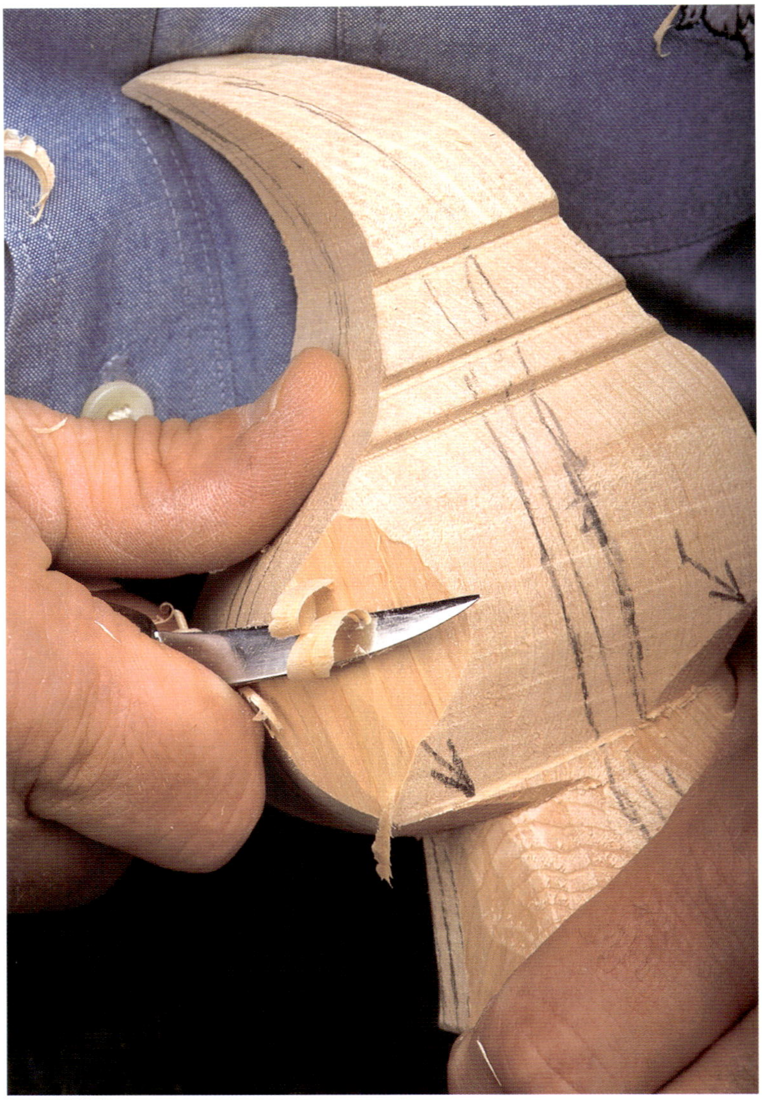

Start to round off the upper body at all four corners.

Round to the flat spot on the left side where the arm will be.

For now we're rounding from the elbows up to the top of the hat.

Be very careful when carving the inside curve of the hat. You will have to turn the carving around and cut from the top of the hat down to avoid cutting off the top of the hat.

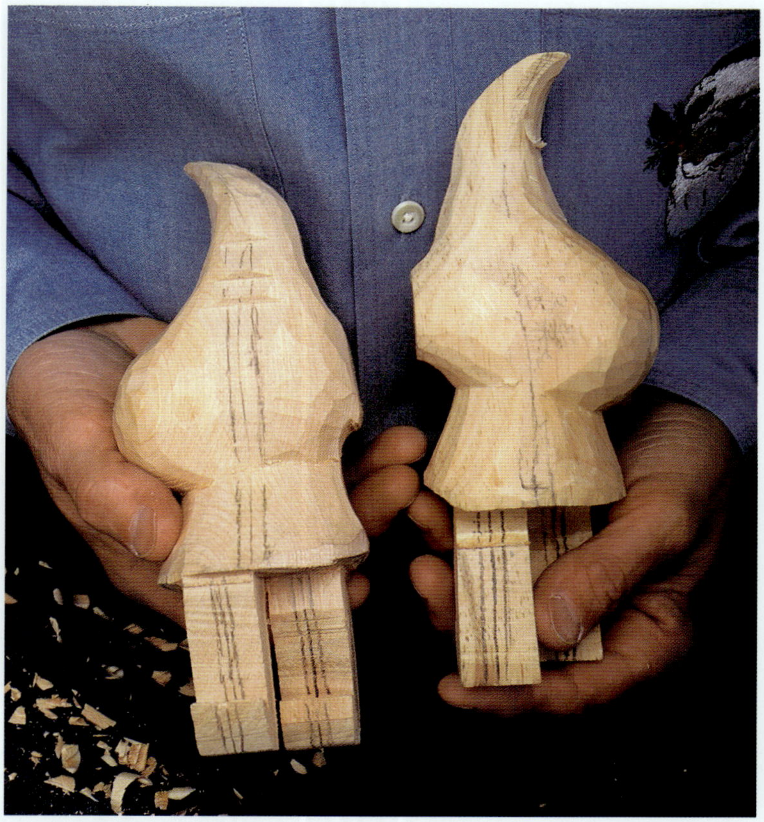

Now you're rounding down from the elbows into the coat to finish the rounding of the body.

Here you see the front and back carved to round.

These two profiles show the beard, hat, and arm. The white pine project on the right shows the addition of fur along the base of the coat and down the center. The beard has more motion to it on the right as well. The white cedar example on the left does not. This is a place where the carver makes the project his or her own.

Using a method I call "double thumbs carving" carve the face and hair up into the hat.

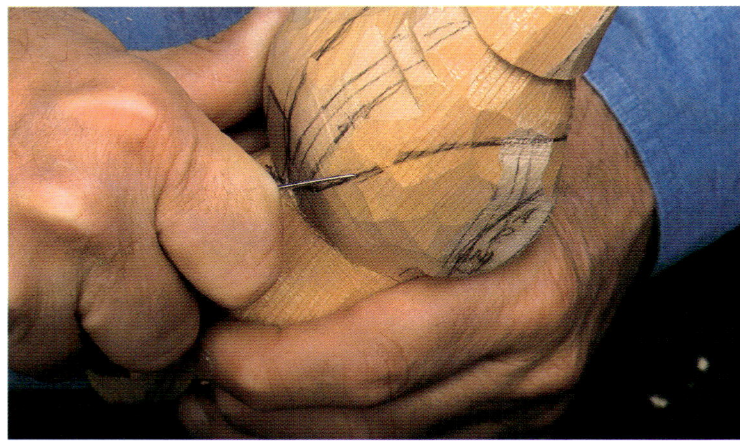

Score around the beard with the knife, cutting straight in.

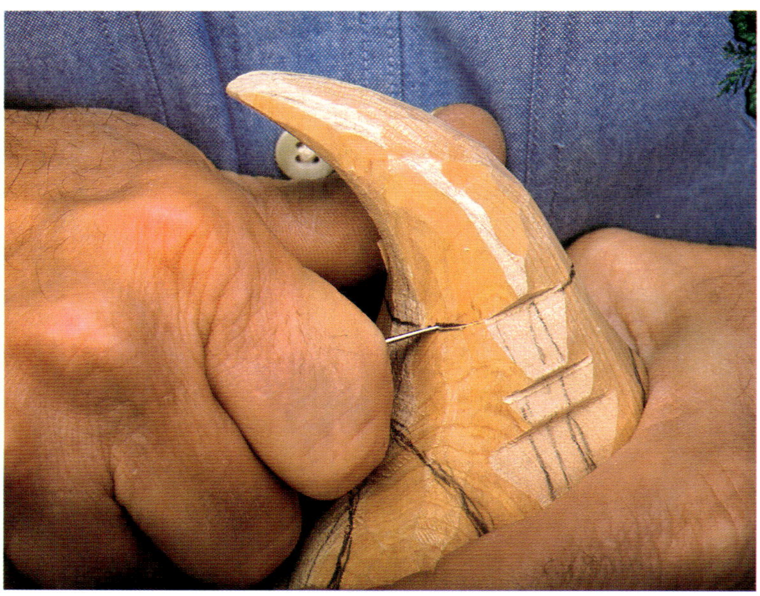

Score a fairly deep line around the brim of the hat.

Relieve from the body to the beard. I like to relieve at least a 1/4" around the beard.

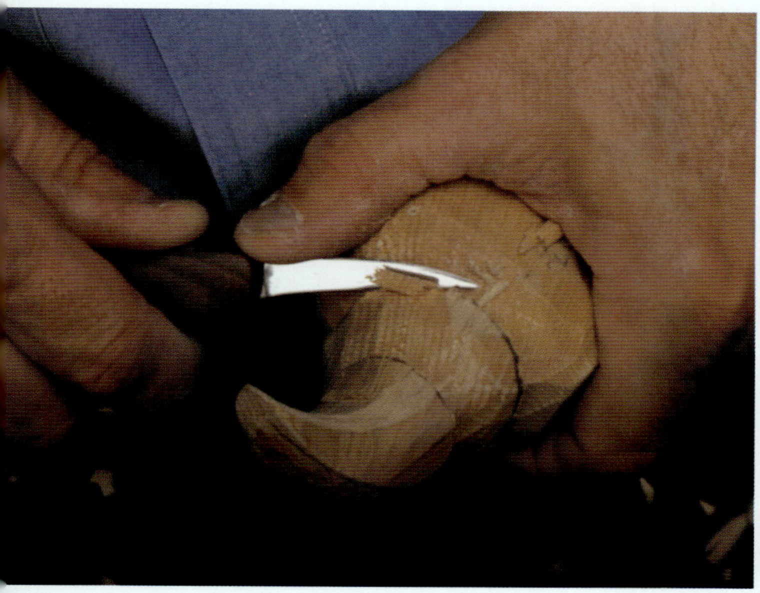

Relieve around the back of the hair, across the shoulders, and into the beard.

The body has been relieved away from the beard and the hair on the back of the head.

The Foredom tool can make the same cuts, relieving material away from the beard and hair with greater speed.

Create a reference line for the right shoulder by aligning it with the carved shoulder on the left. This does not have to be perfect.

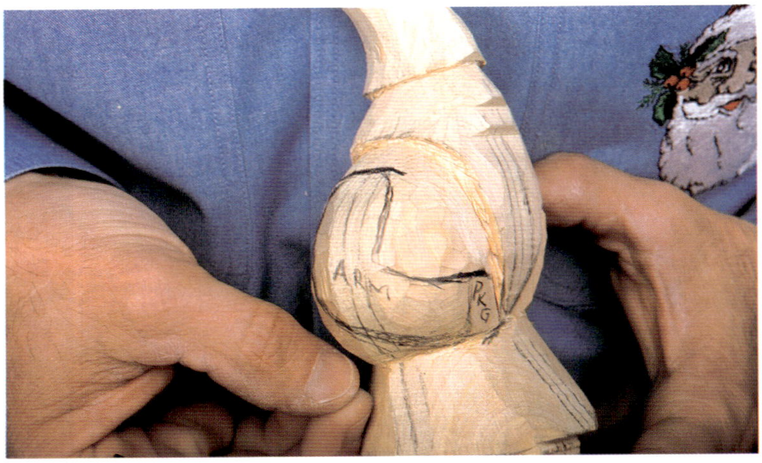

Here is the outline of the right arm, including the package.

When relieving away the excess wood, you'll be carving down toward the forearm and in toward the beard.

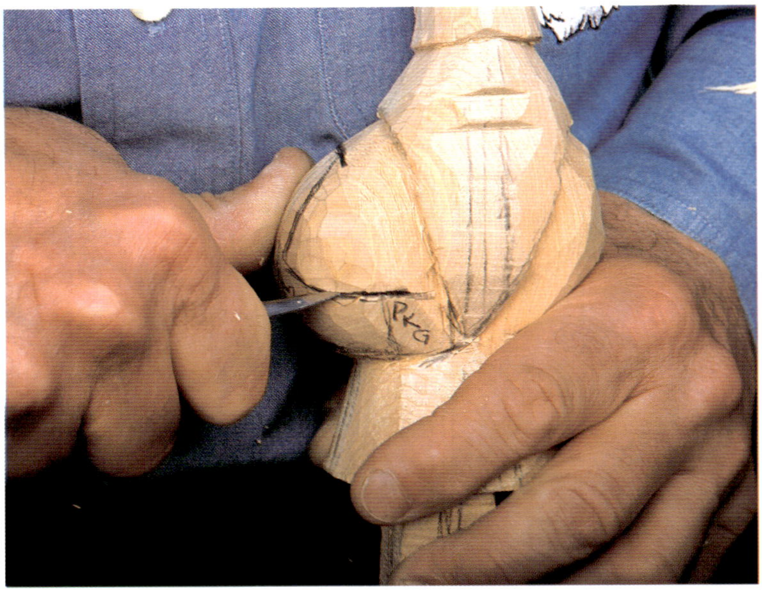

Score the forearm and the package.

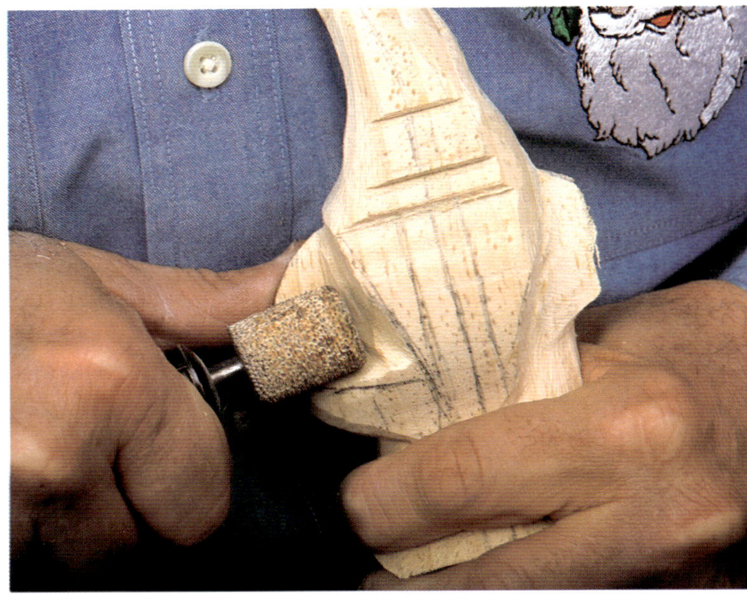

Using the Foredom tool is another, quicker way to remove the excess material.

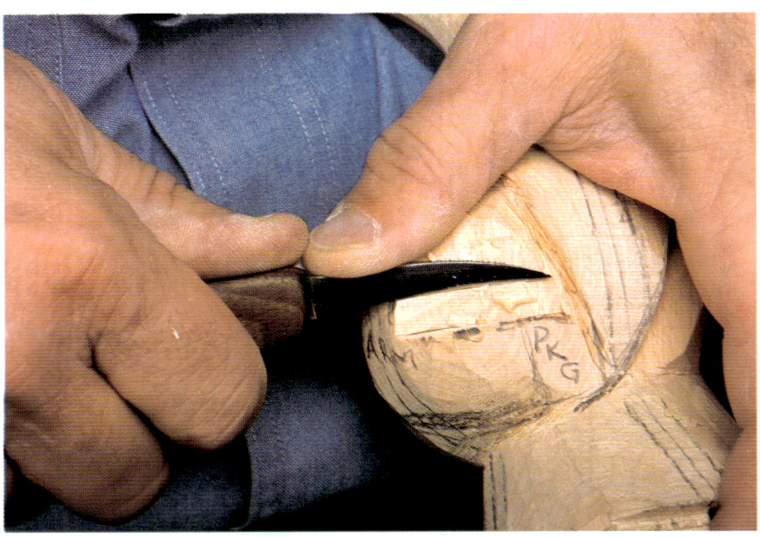

Begin to remove excess wood from above the arm.

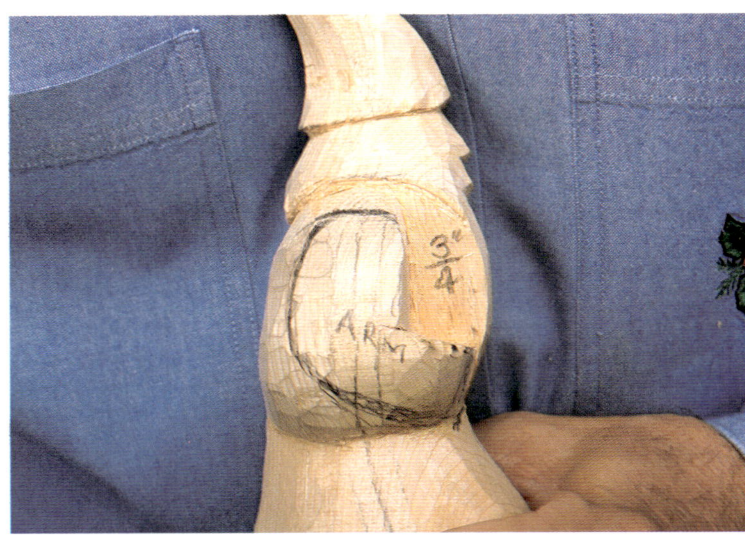

The left arm has been relieved about 3/4" in along the beard line. The upper and lower arm form approximately a 90 degree angle.

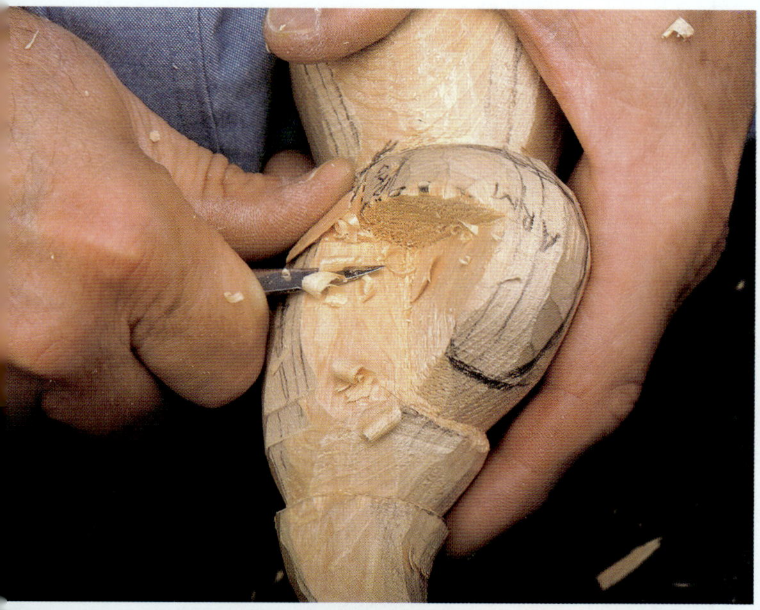

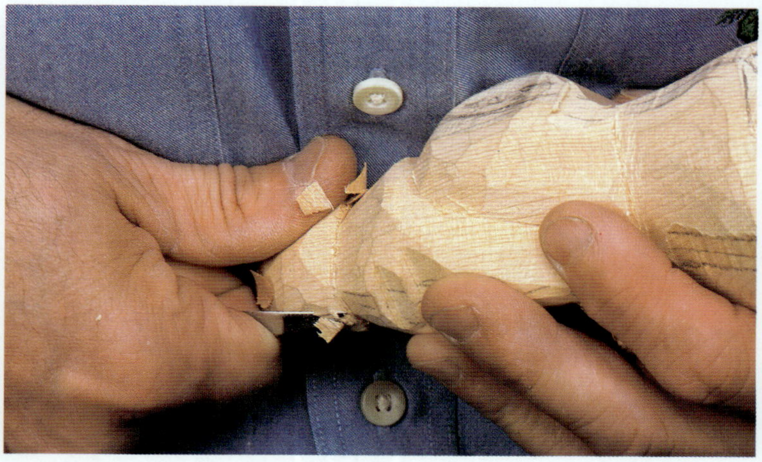

Round the edge of the hat down to the head as well.

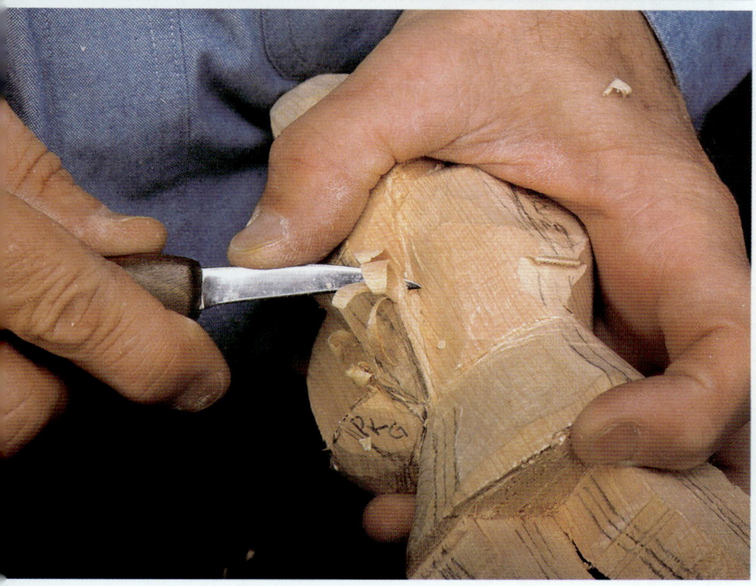

We're rolling the beard from the centerline down. You can leave the beard as round and full as you like.

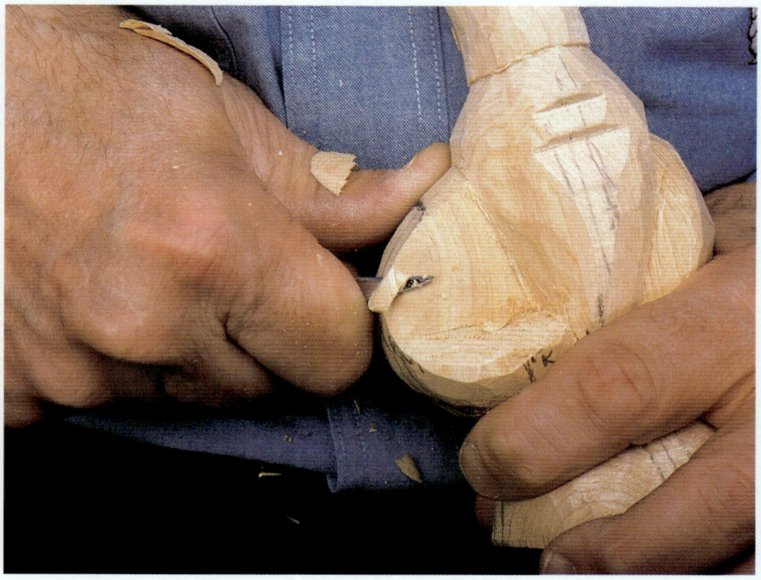

Round the arm.

Round the hair on the back of the head.

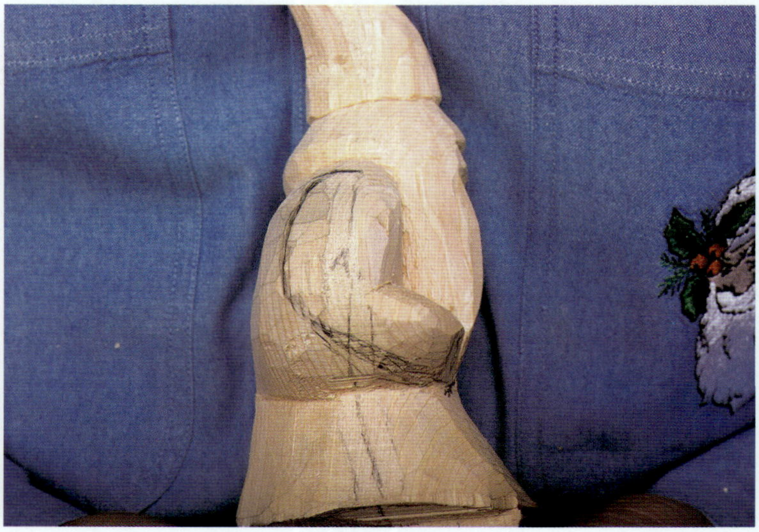

The front of the arm and the shoulder have been rounded.

Now, take some extra time and sharpen your knife because you are going to be cutting across the grain. Round the right arm down and into the back. Round both the top and bottom of the arm.

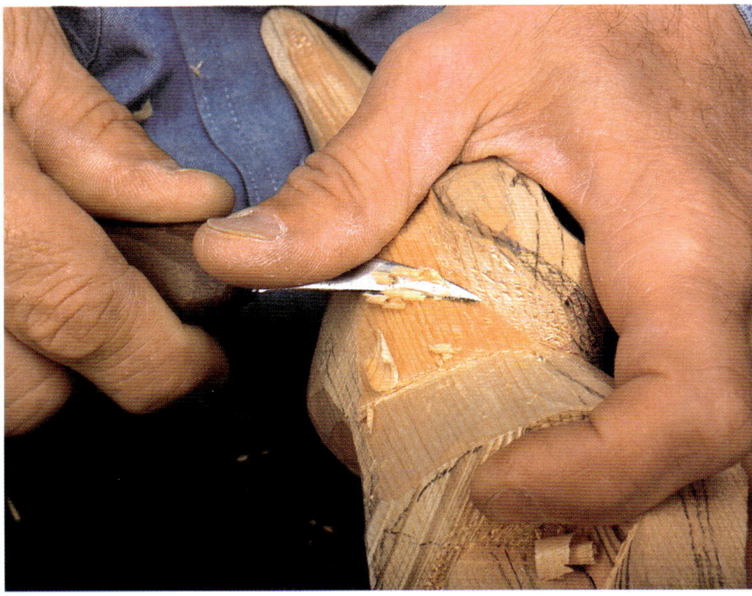

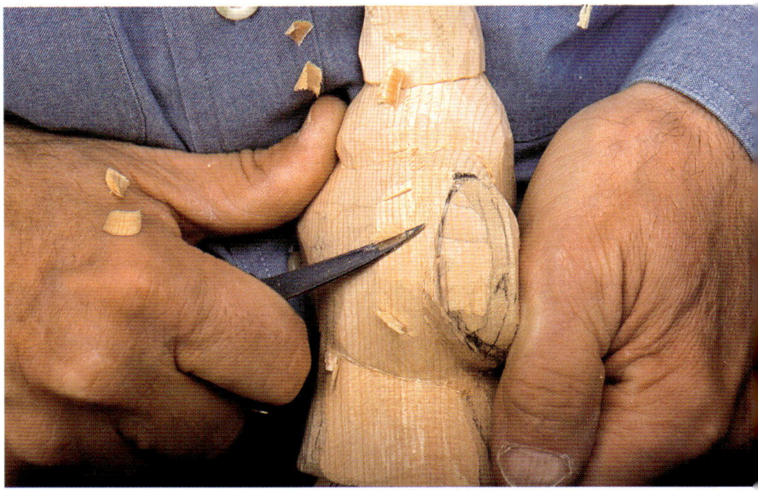

Round the back into the arm.

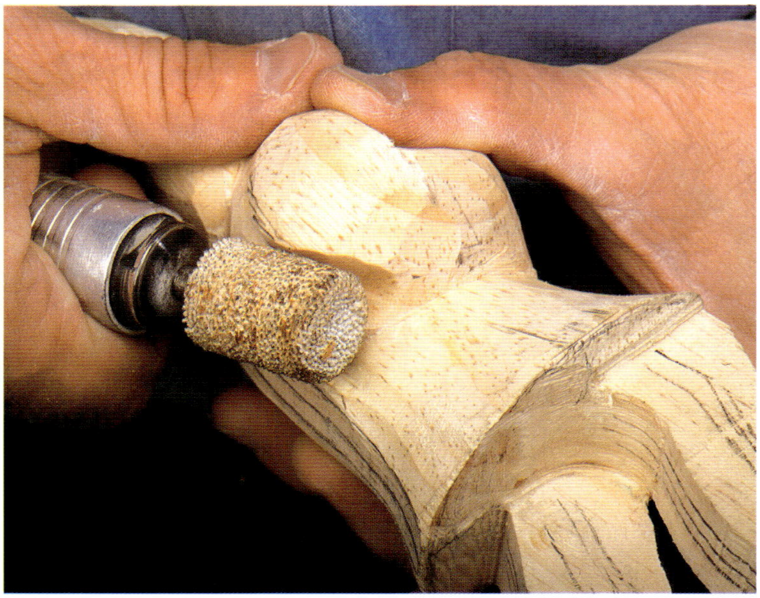

Using the Foredom tool is the easiest way to round the arm into the back.

Take some time to look at the back to make sure that both sides are even.

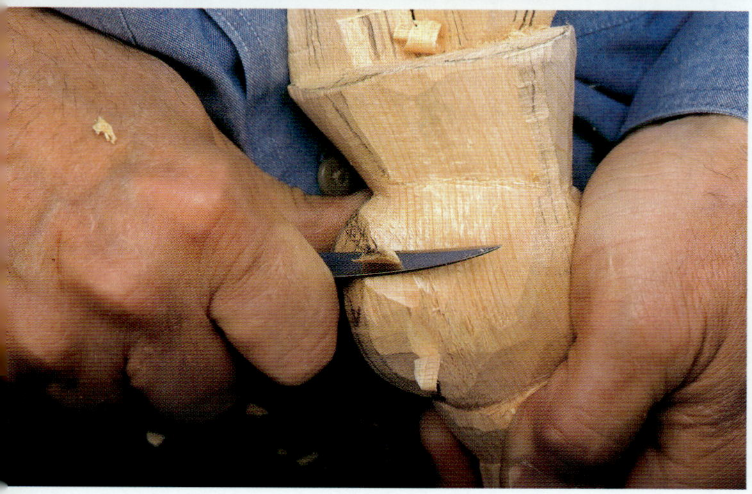

Round over the arm, both above and below the elbow.

Scoop out the material between the beard and the left arm socket, maintaining the flat spot for the left arm.

One of my favorite tools is this hook knife. It removes material from curved inner surfaces very well.

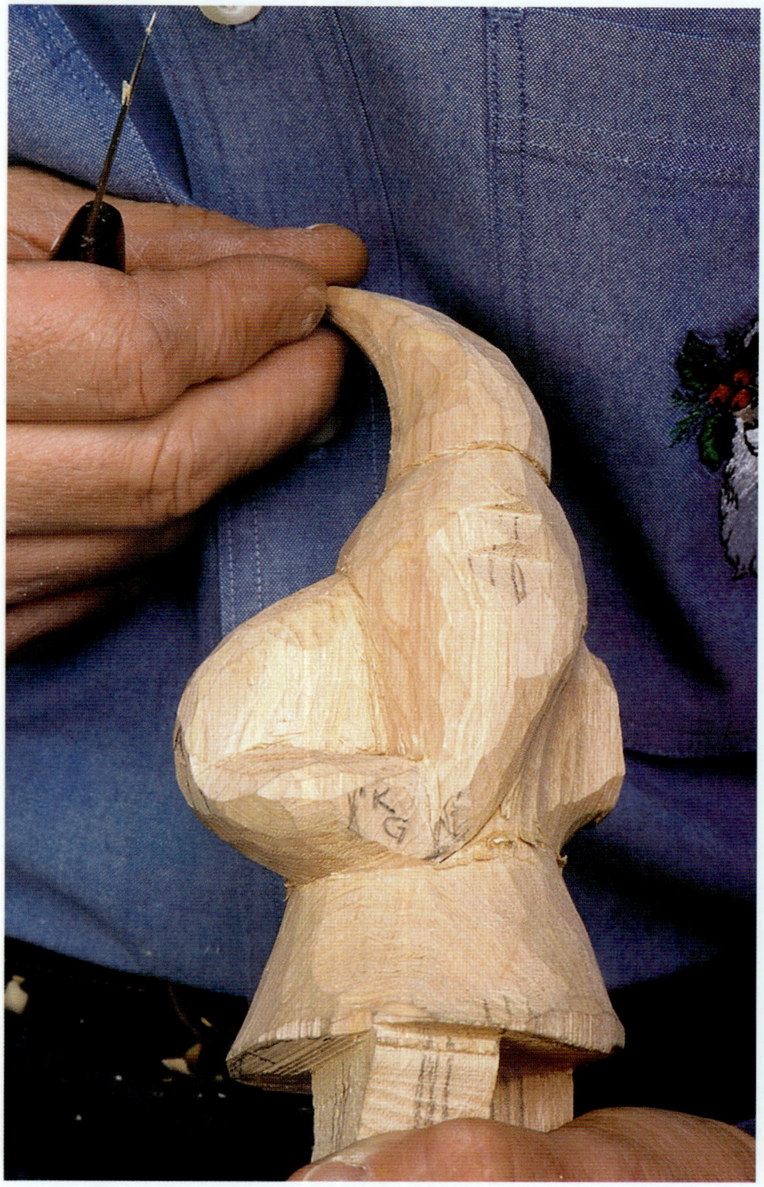

Now take some time to round down the centerlines and clean up the rough spots and excess wood.

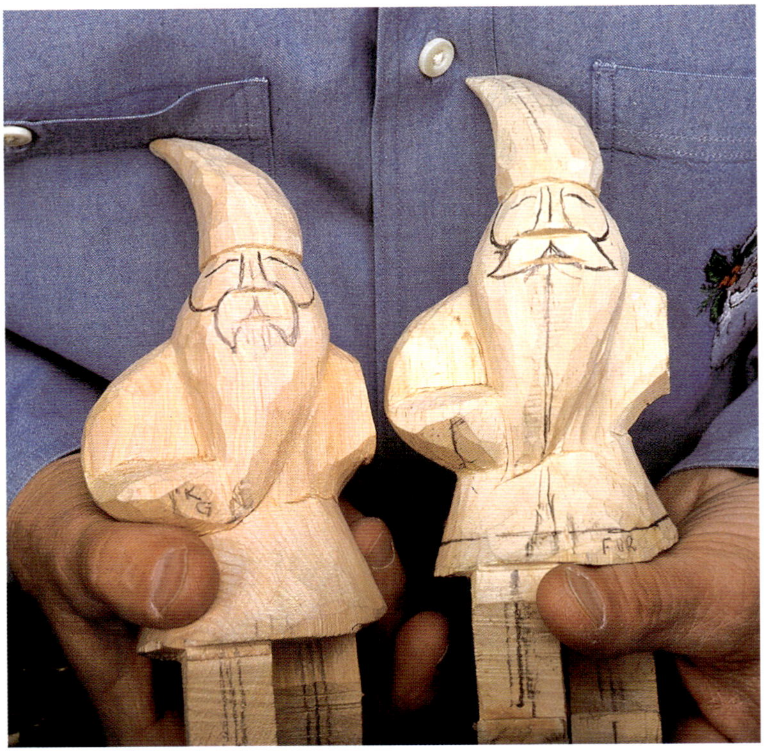

It is time to place some details on the face. You have many options when it comes to layout of the mustache. Draw it however it pleases you. Lay out reference lines for the nose and beard.

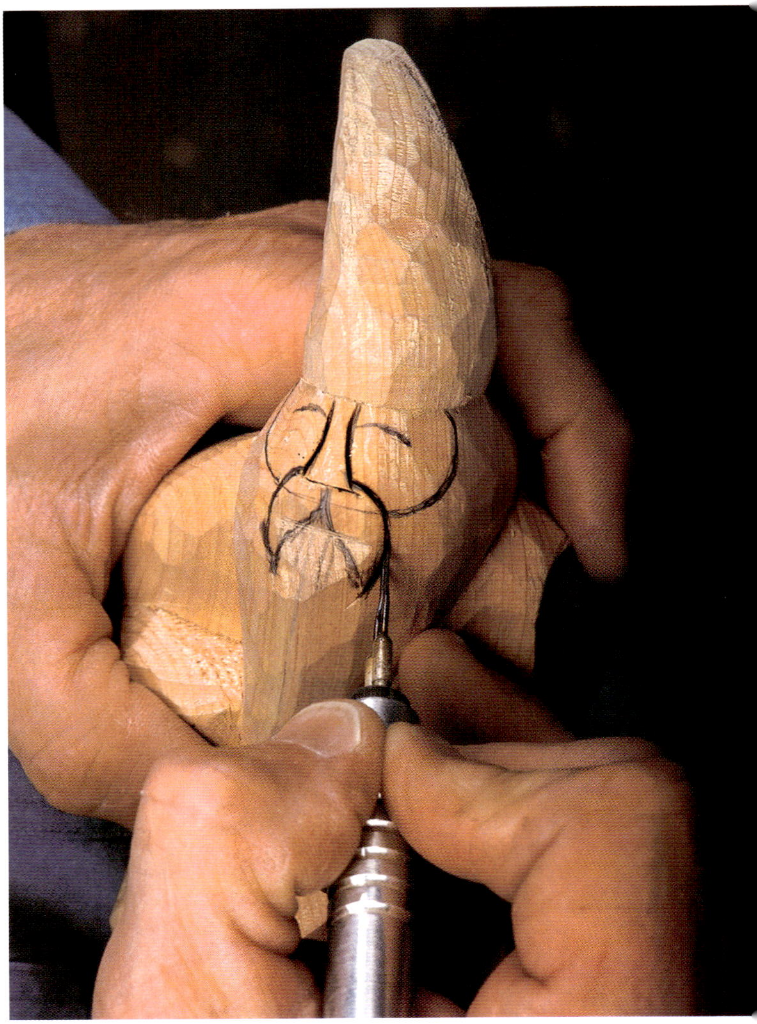

Since I use grainy wood, I like to burn all my fine details in first with a burning pen. The hard grain on a piece of soft wood will sometimes deflect a knife. A burning pen makes it easier to cut the line in. The burning pen isn't a necessity, but it surely helps.

You don't have to use a gauge, but you do need to keep the face symmetrical.

With all the facial lines burned in, you are ready to carve the face. You may notice that I used the burning pen around the brim of the hat to clean up that edge as well.

Start by cutting away the sides of the nose and relieving the top of the mustache.

After you've cut away from your burn line, go back and score. Make sure you cut deep enough that your lines are at the same depth. Remember to go back and sharpen your knife regularly as you work. When carving in this area, remember to keep your knife flat and try hard not to cut up into the beard, mustache, and nose.

Carve away material from the cheek. This needs to be a fairly deep cut because of the texturing we will do later. We also need to be able to roll the beard to make it nice and full and round.

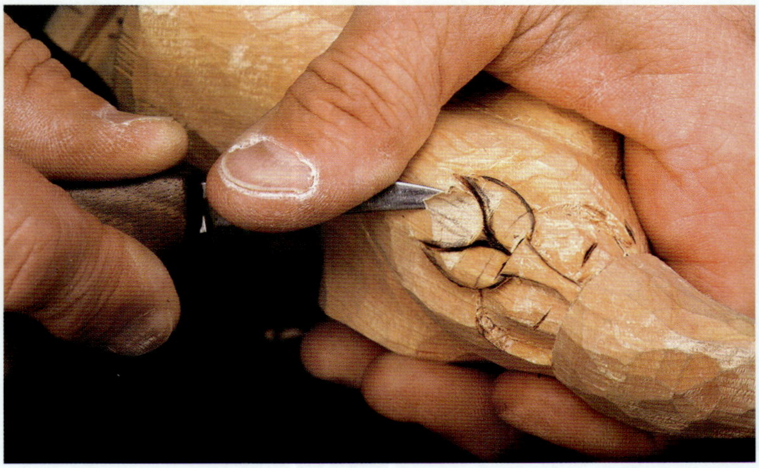

Relieve the area inside the mustache.

Relieve the outside edge of the mustache first.

The nose, cheeks, and mustache have been relieved.

The outer edge of the mustache has been rolled down. Move on to the inside edge.

Relieve the beard into the cheeks.

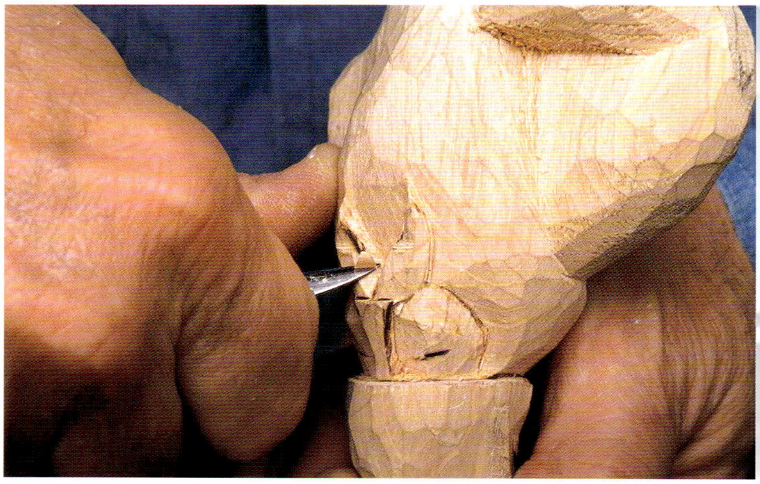

Rolling down the inner edge of the mustache.

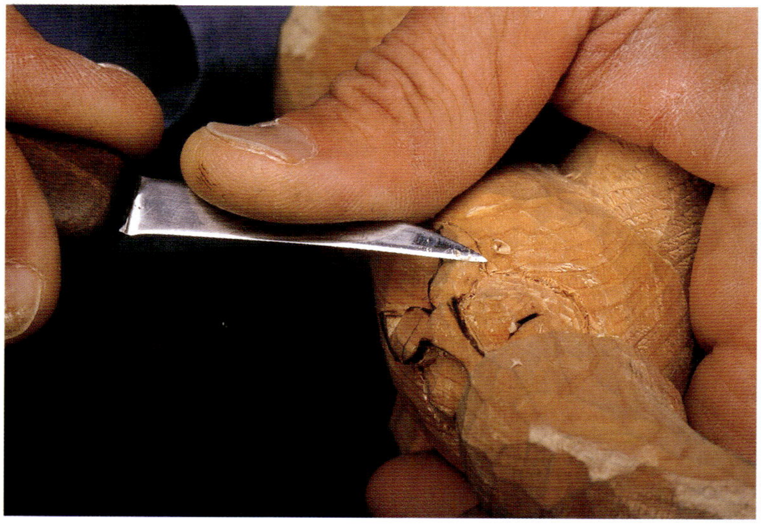

Roll the outside edge of the mustache down to the face and the beard.

The mustache has been rolled down, rounded on inner and outer edges.

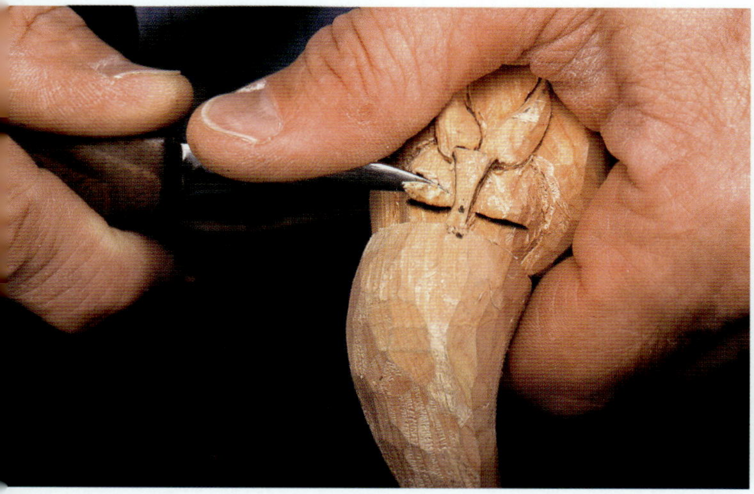

Reestablish your eye line. You probably carved a good bit of it away working on the cheeks and nose. Make a V cut into the eye line that has been burned in.

The bridge of the nose is cut in. The shape of the nose is now established.

The second cut comes from the eyebrow down (the burned in line) to complete the V cut and the eye.

Cut in the bridge of the nose.

Add some definition to the side of the eye channel by making a V cut along the outer edge of each eye.

The V cut is in place.

I'm using a diamond bit to smooth the features of the face, getting rid of all the hard and angular lines.

Add some crow's feet in this area to both eyes.

The face is now round and smooth.

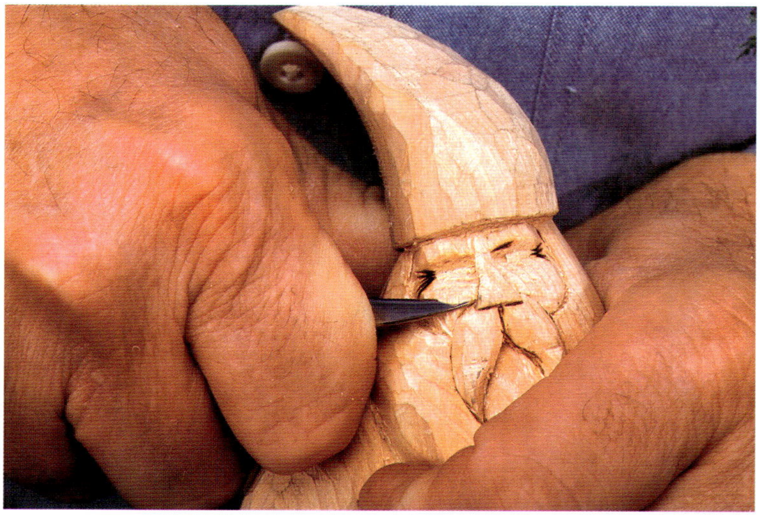

Round over the cheeks, evening them up and rounding over corners.

Shape the brim of the hat back into the face and hair.

The hat is now rolled into the face and the hair.

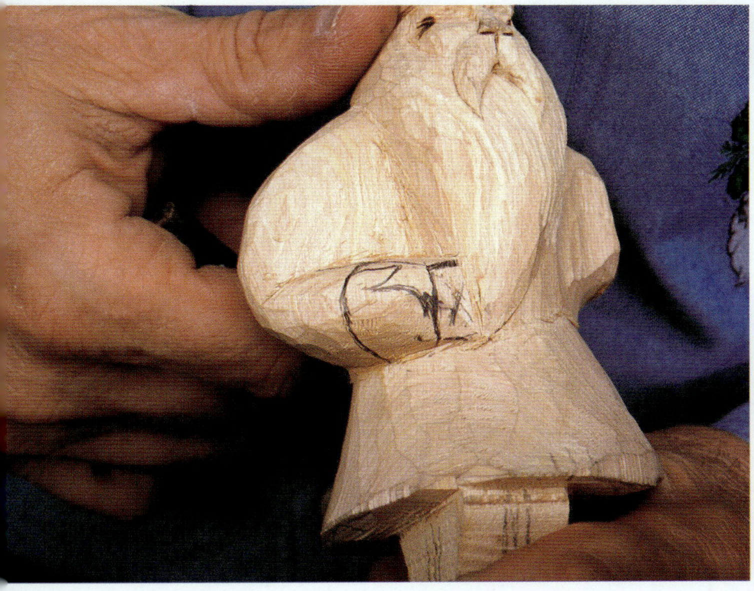

I have outlined the right arm with the package and the mitten.

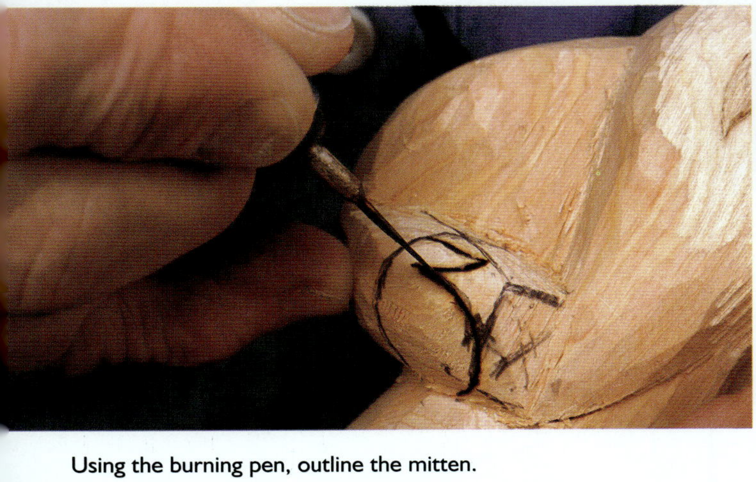

Using the burning pen, outline the mitten.

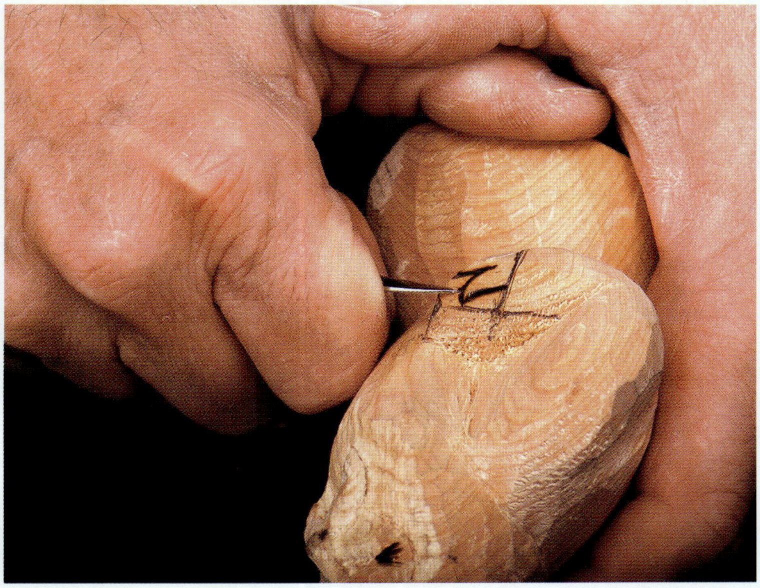

Take time to sharpen your knife now. Make your stop cut along the thumb. Cut down vertically along the edge of the package toward the thumb. Be patient here or you will take the thumb off.

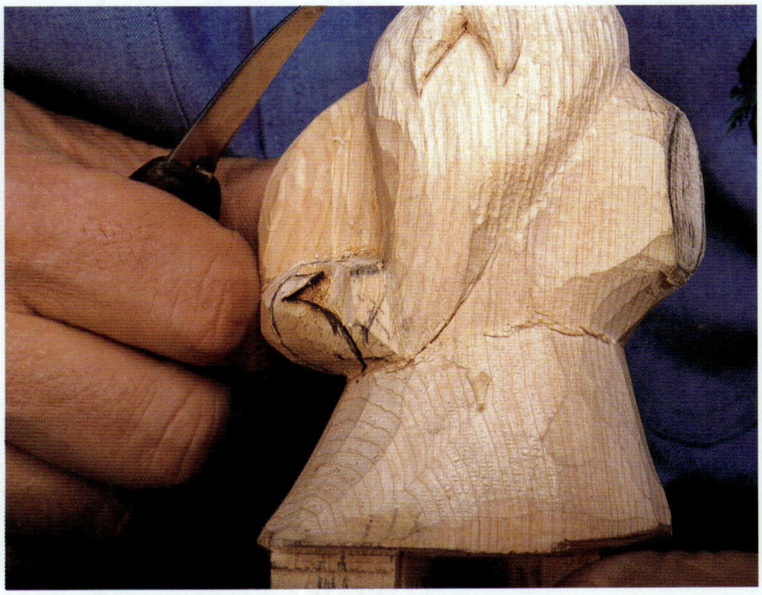

We've relieved the mitten about 1/8" off the package.

Round down the mitten to the package.

Score the center line for the coat.

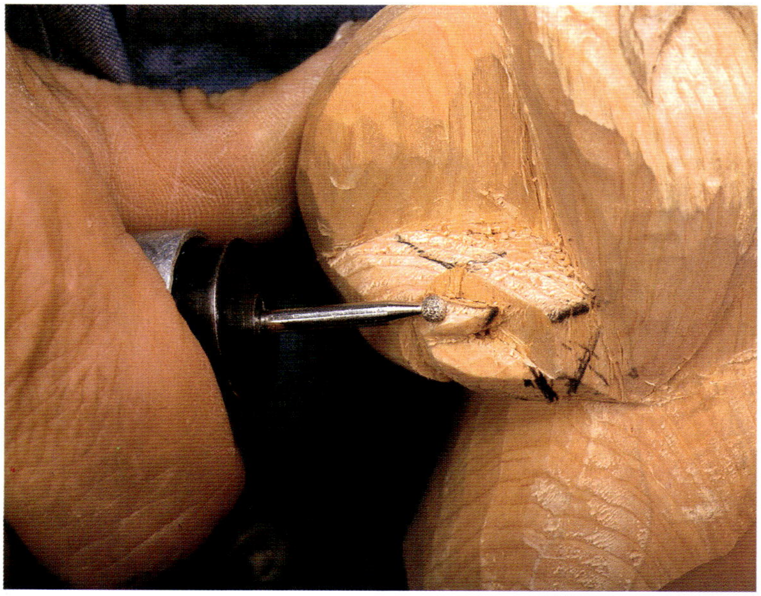

Use your diamond bit to smooth out your mitten.

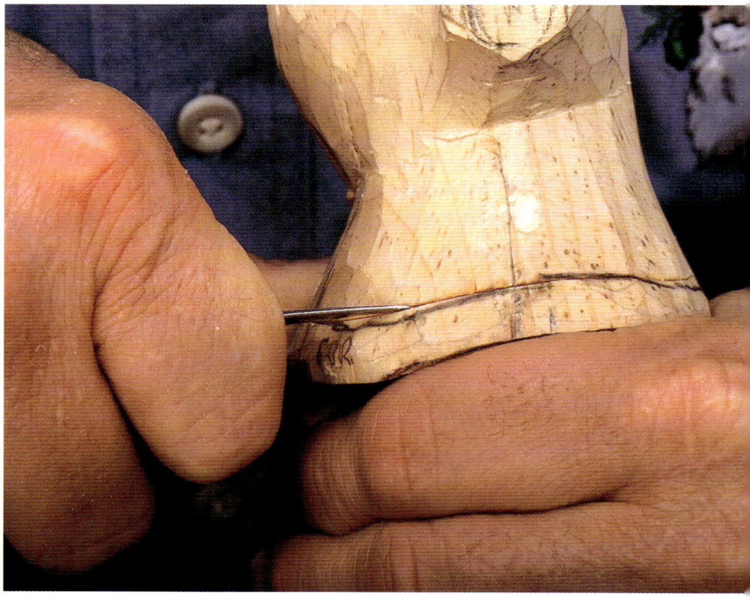

Score the fur at the base of the coat and up the center of the coat.

Relieve on the left hand side of the coat.

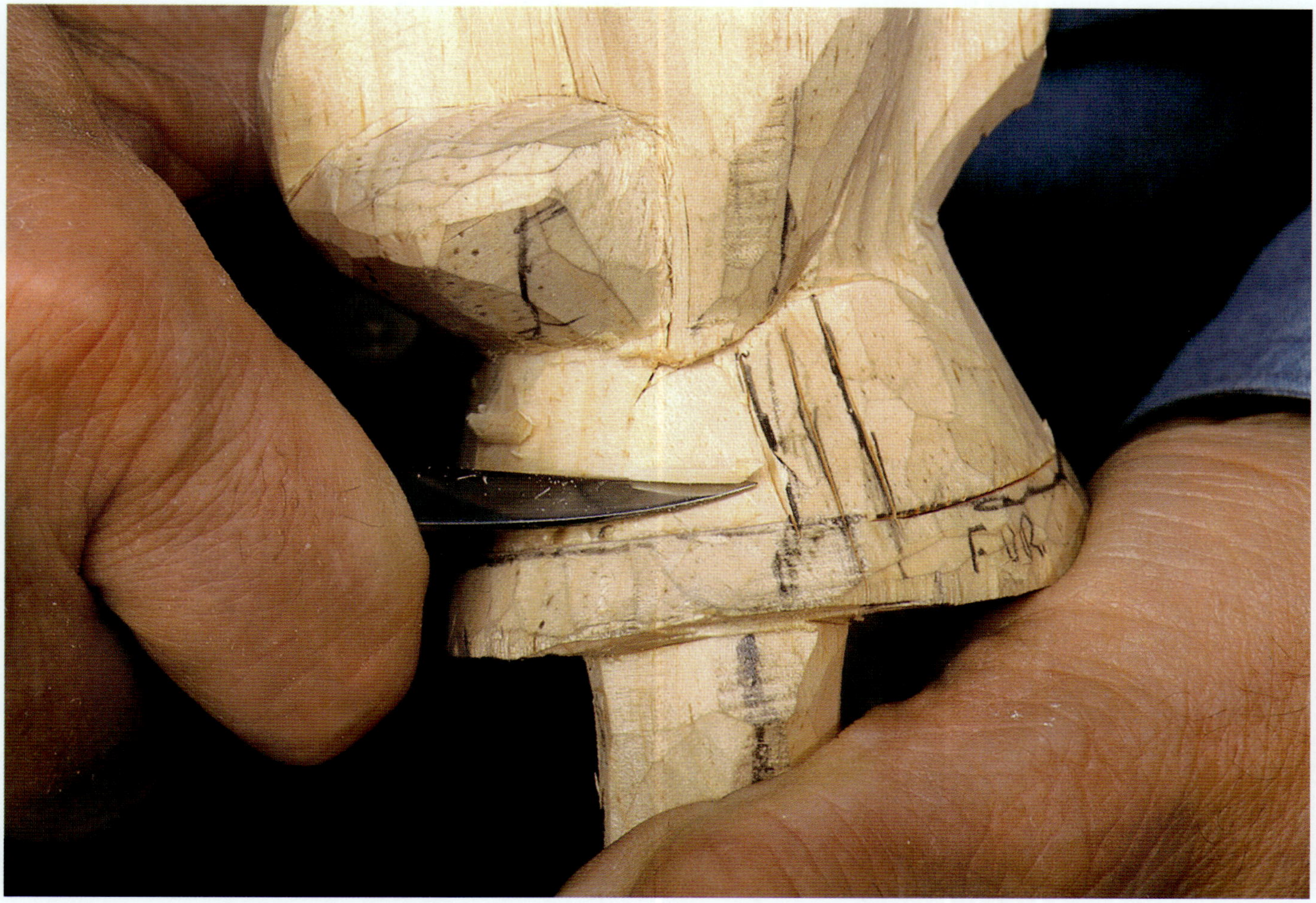

Relieve material away around the fur, leaving the fur raised above the surface of the coat.

Layout a rough shape of the bottom of the boot.

If you decided to have pointed toe shoes or boots, my suggestion is add fast and hard drying cyanoacrylate glue to (i.e. Super Glue) the tips now so that they don't break off when you are carving. If you notice any checks or hairline cracks in the bottoms of your boots, legs, or anywhere else on your carving, add cyanoacrylate glue. It tends to stop any further checking.

As wood dries, shrinkage occurs, causing cracks or checks (lines) on the end grain of stock. Cyanoacrylate glue will hold the wood tight.

Proceed with the legs just like the rest of the body, carving from centerline to centerline, rounding out the legs.

Rounding the legs.

Now is a good time to make sure the leg thickness is the same.

The legs are rounded. It is time for details. As far as detailing the legs, boots and/or shoes, you are only limited by your imagination. Burn in the top of the boot and round the pant leg down into the top of the boot.

Around both legs, on all sides, keep the knife blade flat to the base of the coat and make stop cuts into the legs.

The pant leg is rounded down.

Cut off the excess from the toe of the boot. You may need to reapply cyanoacrylate glue once the toe has been reduced. I know I do.

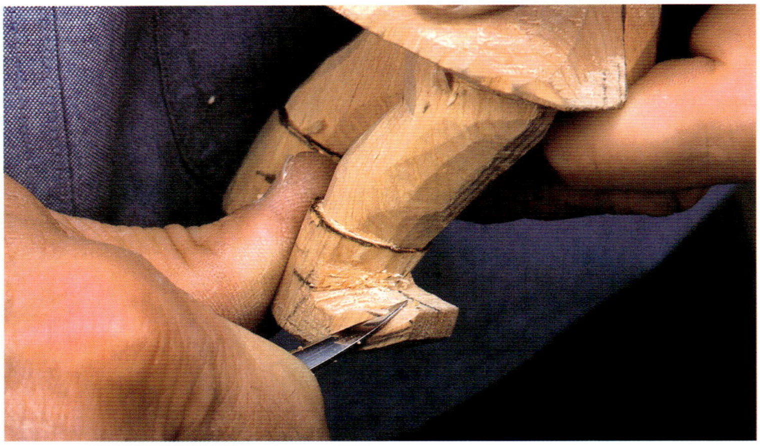

I am scooping out on either side of the boot.

Establish the shape of the toe.

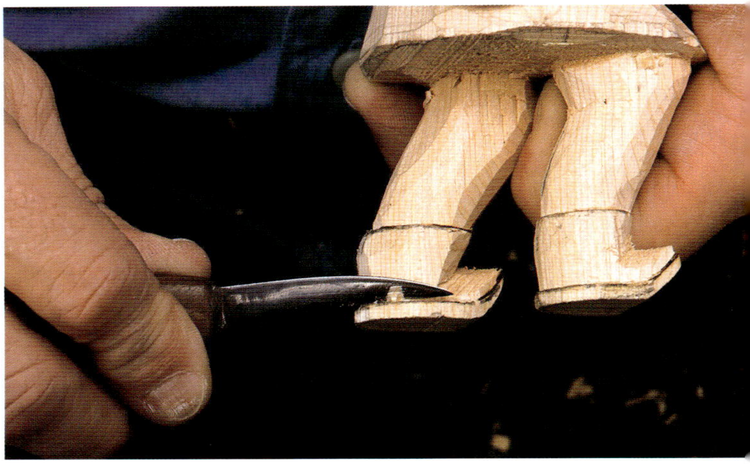

To add detail to the boot, draw and burn in the sole. Use your knife to reduce the boot back away from the sole.

The feet are complete. If you like you can use a stone and go over the rough edges to smooth them down.

Now it is time to carve the left arm. Use your arm patterns on a 3" x 2 1/2" x 1 3/4" piece of carving stock. In this case I am using white cedar. It is very important to lay out the arm with the grain.

Now cut the top profile.

Drill a hole inside the elbow. Use your band saw to cut out the arm. Note: you are not going to be able to cut a lot of detail into the hand. Don't worry about this. You will also place a dab of hot glue in the corners.

Lay out centerlines and some reference lines on all sides of the arm. This arm is oversized to allow you options in changing the shape of the arm, allowing for a fur cuff if you wish to include one.

Round down the arm.

I like to leave plenty of excess around the joint where the arm attaches to the shoulder until I decide exactly how to place the arm.

Before you attach the missing arm, go over the completed figure and remove any high spots and pencil lines, balance the beard, and remove any band saw lines.
With that done, I'm balancing the left arm to my right arm to determine where the cuff will go prior to carving the mitten holding the walking stick. Remember that this arm is currently bigger than it needs to be.

Cut the mitten into the sleeve along the sleeve line.

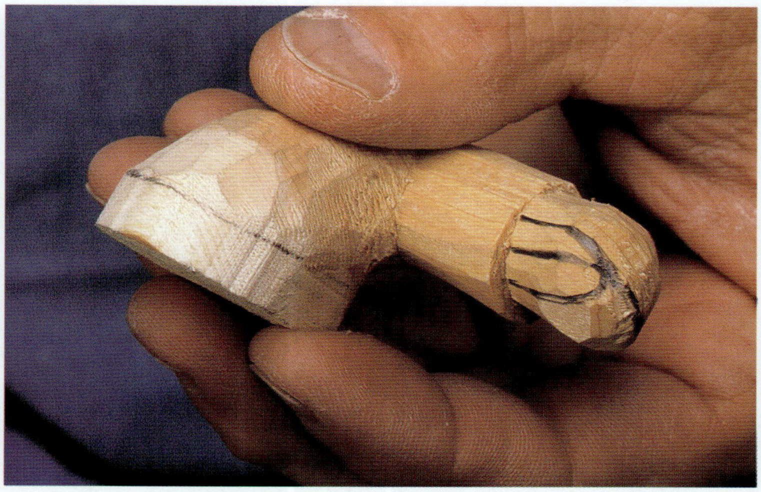

I've drawn in the position of the mitten and the enclosing thumb. The thumb needs to be a bit oversized.

We've rounded down the hand into the sleeve. We've rounded down the sleeve as well to match the arm holding the package.

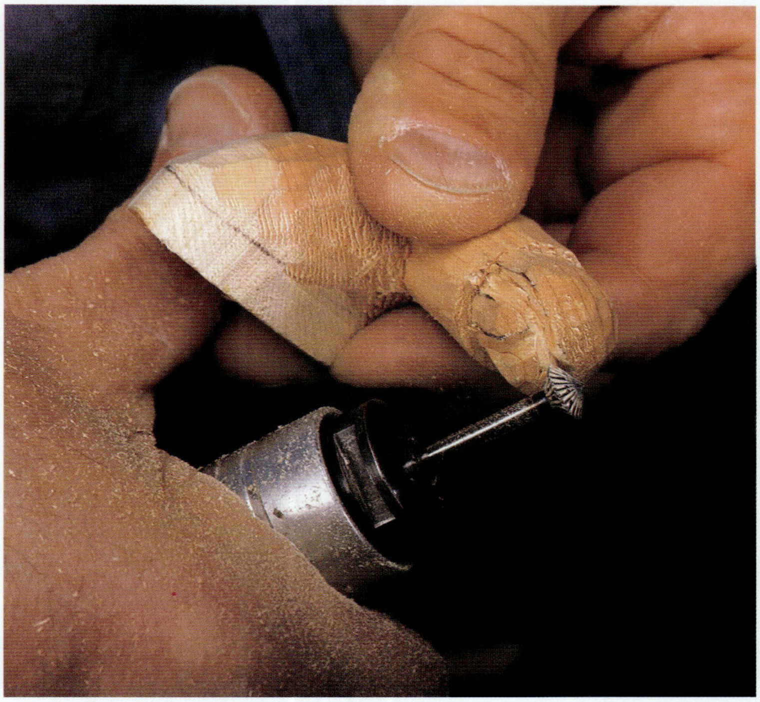

I use the V bit to establish the thumb and mitten. Establishing the thumb and mitten.

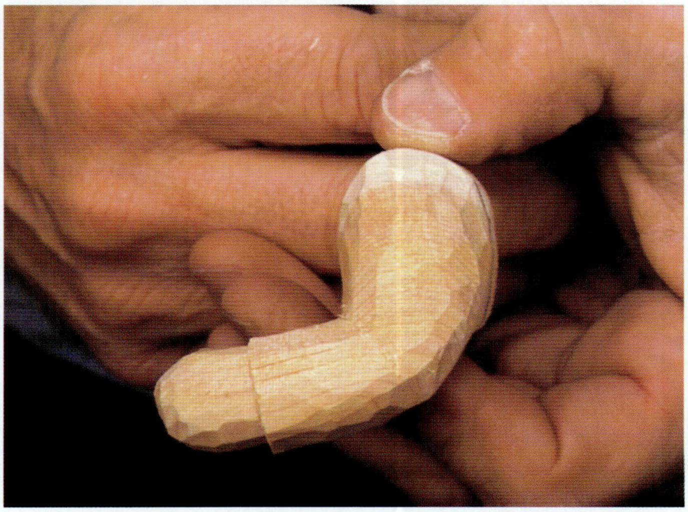

I use the diamond stone to round out the bottom of the V cut.

Make a fairly deep cut at the crook in the arm to create a crease in the fabric of the sleeve.

Use your knife to remove some of the excess material below the thumb. Caution: you will need enough wood below the thumb to keep the walking stick in place.

We've left lots of excess wood on the back of the arm as this gives you lots of option on final arm placement.

Do a little fine tuning on the sleeve at this time.

Here is the position of the arm (tucked in or swung out depending on how you cut the arm).

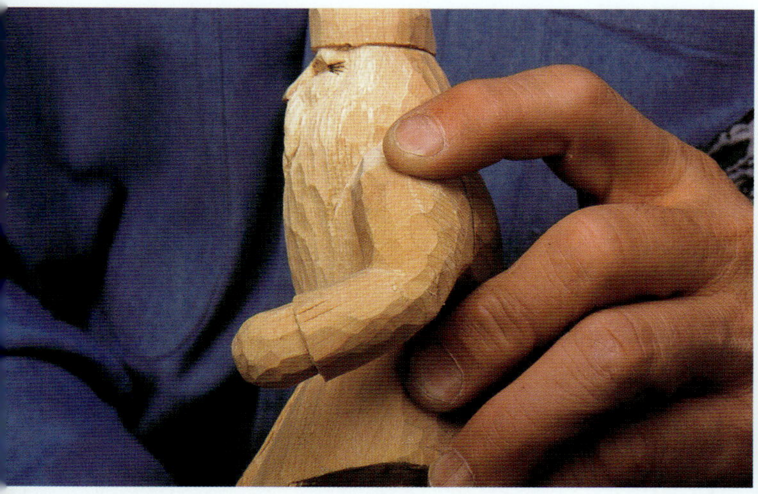

One of the options, with the arm placed low.

In this shot, I've taken a little more off the arm to place it out a little and center it in the middle of the body. Notice that the body and the arm do not meet exactly under the arm. You will have to go back in after the glue dries and carve the body and arm together as one.

A small depression on the back side of the arm and shoulder does two things for you. It allows more surface area for your glue and it usually allows for a little tighter fit as you have gotten rid of some high spots.

To attach the arm to the shoulder, I use an expanding polyurethane glue. I use the expanding glue as it is a gap filler and it cures with moisture present. You may notice the back of the arm is a little wet.

I use rubber bands to secure the arm first. They also act as a cushion for the clamps.

Once the glue is dried, carve the underside of the arm into the body.

Remember to keep your stock square. Before cutting out the front profile, establish a slight taper at the bottom of the pack on the side view. Cut out the front profile. A dab of hot glue in the corners secures the side pattern in place long enough to cut the side profile out on the band saw.

Now that the arm is in place, lay out the pattern for the rucksack on a 2 1/2" x 1 1/2" x 3" block of wood. Experience has taught me to use a very grainy piece of cedar. Pine also works well, but tupelo gum does not. Try to find the tightest grained wood you can. Make sure you lay out the pattern with the grain.

The front and side profiles of the rucksack have been cut. Establish your centerlines.

Add a few lines to the bottom as well.

Carve from the center up to the top and from the center down to the bottom when rounding the rucksack.

After the rucksack has been carved to round, this is one of the very few parts of my carvings that I sand. Then I add the reference lines. I draw the lines about 3/16" to 1/4" apart. I mark the top (about 1/8" to 3/16") parallel to the outside.

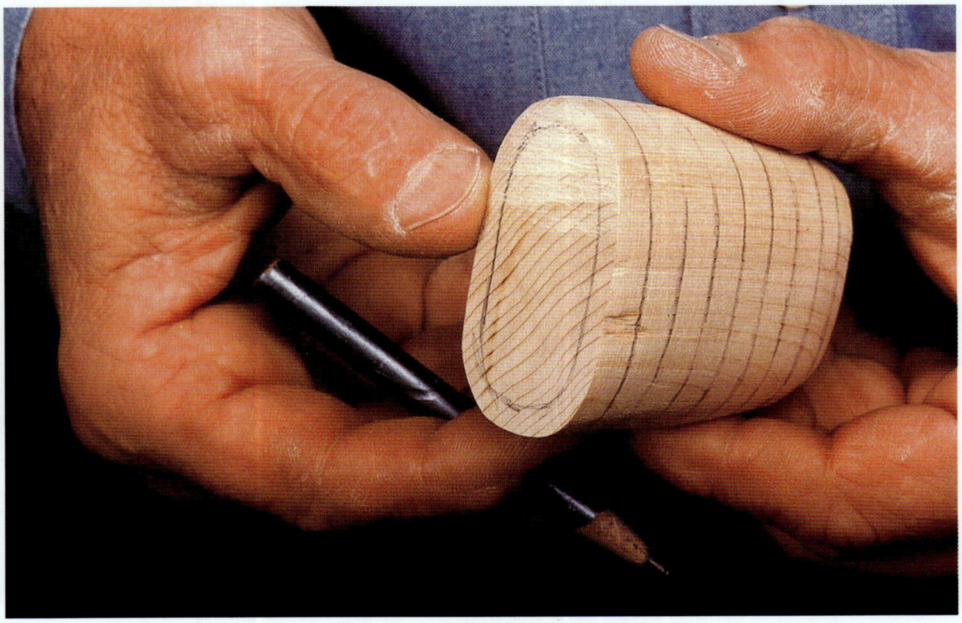

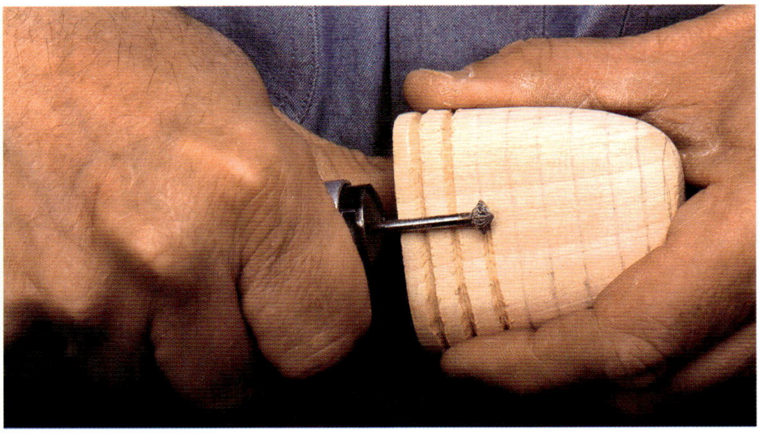

Using this V bit I found at a carving show, I cut in on each line to create the impression of a basket weave. Don't be afraid to make these cuts fairly deep. The texturing we will do later needs a deep cut.

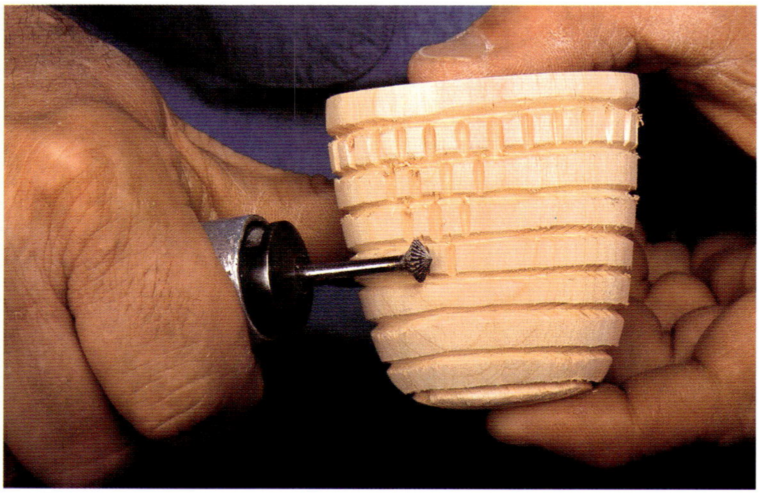

For my vertical cuts, I use the same V bit, cutting in vertical lines, spaced about 3/16" apart. To create the effect of a basket weave, the next line of vertical cuts is spaced on center with the first cuts. Repeat the pattern to the bottom.

The basket weave pattern is complete.

There are several ways to make a hole in the top of your basket. You can use a drill, or a Phingst™ carbide bit, to remove wood from the interior of the basket. This bit can be very aggressive. Be careful.

To create the illusion at the top of the basket, I use a much thinner disk, at a slight angle around the rim.

The basket is finished.

Wood with straight grain is easy to work ... however, it is dull. Like a wrinkled human face, a gnarled piece of wood is more interesting ... it has character. It is of course harder to work with, but the results are worth the effort. Pass the stock through the 5/16" hole. Hold the stick high toward the top and gently tap straight down, driving the wood through.

To create a walking stick, it is best to use wood with a noticeable grain such as oak, pine, walnut, cedar, or maple. The choice of wood is up to you. Just have plenty on hand. You'll need it. The finished stick should be about 6 1/2" long. I usually start with raw stock about 10" long, 5/16" square (you can start larger if you like). The extra inches in length allow for some breakage to occur during reduction of the shaft. Don't be discouraged if your first walking stick breaks (be surprised if it doesn't!). You cannot use twigs or sticks from the backyard to carve a walking stick. A twig has a soft, pithy center that will not stand up well under the stress of carving. I start my walking sticks by tapering one end slightly with a pencil sharpener (a blunt point will do). If you don't have a pencil sharpener, just carve one end down. Shown in the picture is my original walking stick jig made from an electric box. My new jig is a piece of 3/16" steel with holes from 5/16" down to 3/16" by 5/64" increments.

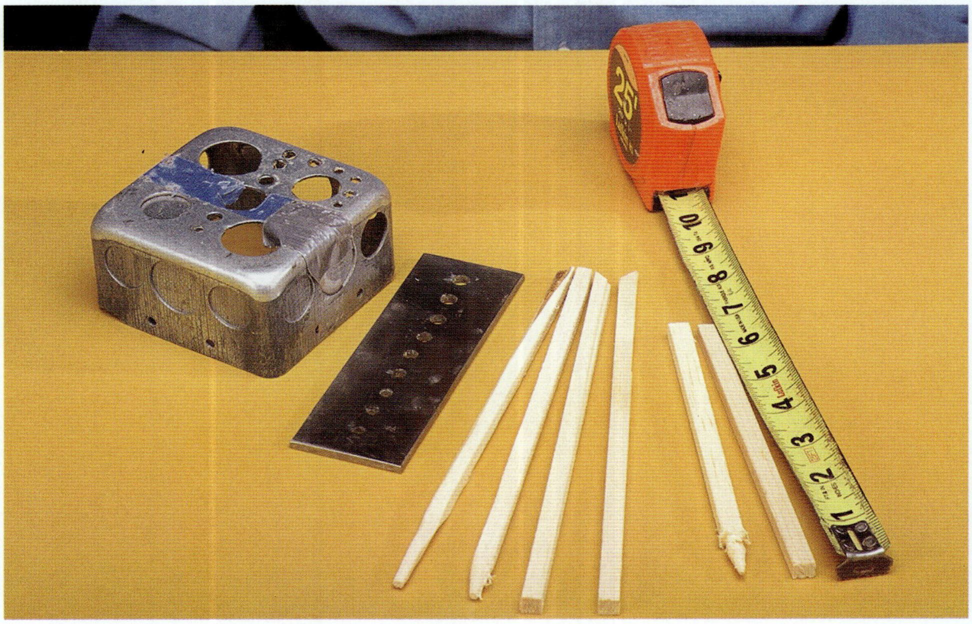

Repeat until you have worked the stock through each hole. Because you are driving the wood through the hole, you are cutting with the grain and your stock will tend to follow. I only drive my stock down to the 3/16" hole, even though I drill a 1/8" hole in the hand to hold the walking stick. I like to have some extra wood at the top and carve down the shaft to fit the hand.

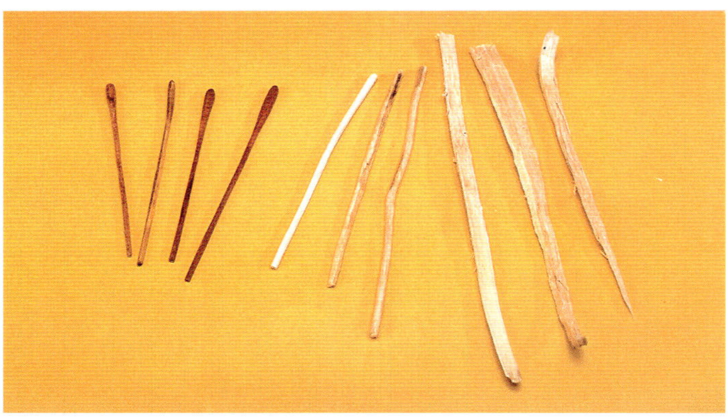

The best walking sticks come from your wood pile. They are the most natural looking. A smart, natural looking walking stick complements your figure and adds significantly to the end result of the project. Break off some narrow strips of wood with some irregular grain. Cutting with your band saw defeats the purpose of the irregular grain. So use your knife to cut the stock down to 3/8" square. This can be a little bit tricky, but you follow the same steps as just shown for reducing the size of this stick. This picture shows rough stock, roughly shaped sticks, and finished walking sticks. You determine the shape at the top of your walking stick.

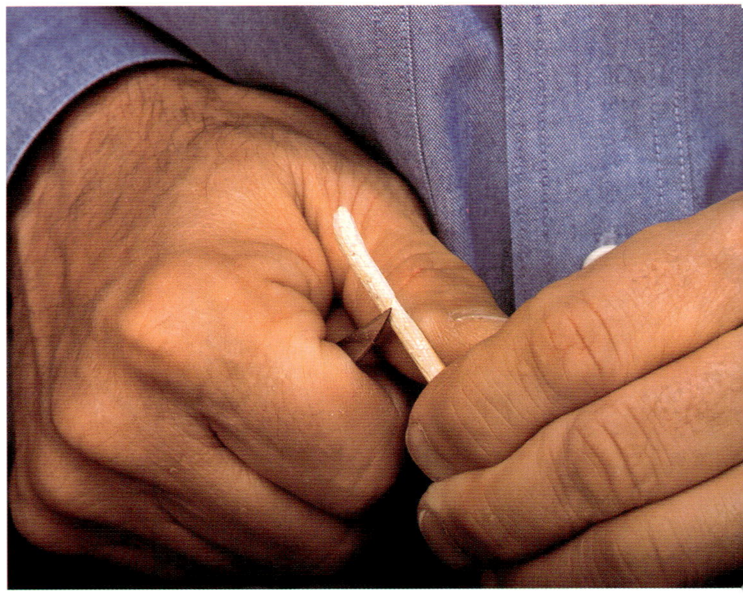

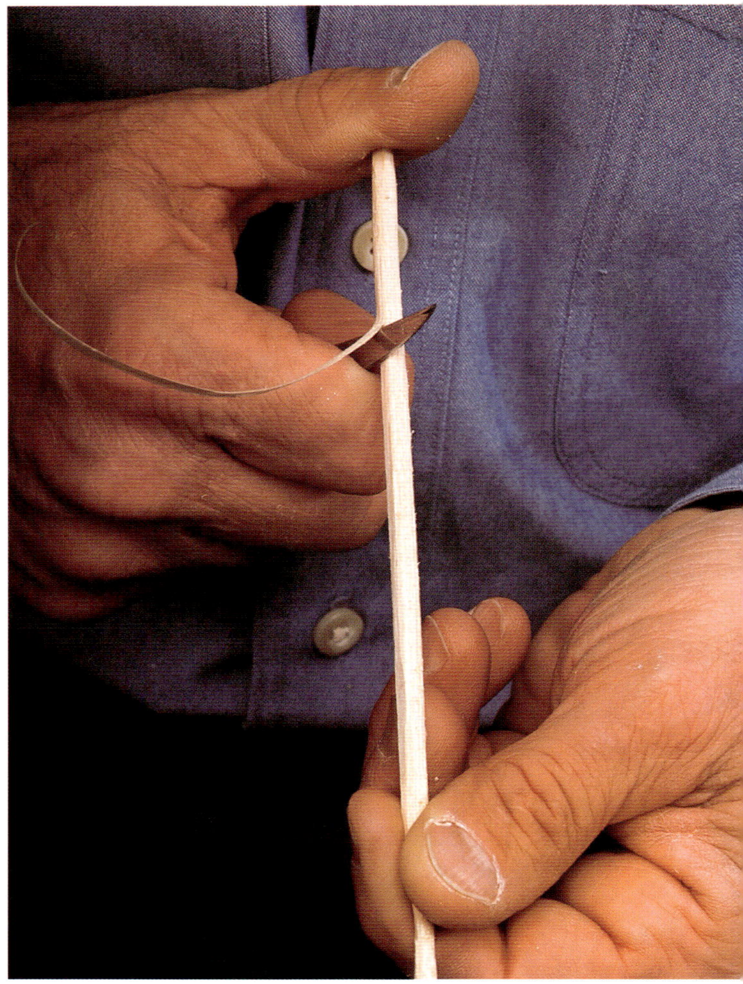

Shaping the top and tapering the shaft. Taper the shaft down to about 1/8". When carving the shaft, remember you have an irregular grain. Do not cut too deeply or you will take off too much.

Wrap sand paper around the shaft to finish reducing the stick to fit in the hand. Lightly sand the top.

Using the Foredom tool and the hook knife, I create the effect of wind-whipped snow, making small ridges and valleys to portray minor drifts. You should have a fairly smooth surface when you are finished creating your ridges. Snow drifts do not have rough edges.

Moving on to the base, I set my band saw between 30 and 45 degrees and I freeform my base with some irregular curves. The shape of the base is entirely up to you. I am using white pine, but any wood you choose should work. You may want to use a highly decorative piece of hardwood. I am using the soft wood because I am going to texture it.

The finished base is carved and ready for texturing, snow, tree, and Jultomten.

I generally use scrap wood for my Christmas tree, whatever nice soft wood I have left over. The size of the tree is determined by the size of my scraps. Methods for tree carving are the same as for any other pattern. Cut out your two profiles and carve to shape. Be imaginative as you carve your tree.

Jultomten's gifts are wrapped with rounded edges and secured with string. Where the strings cross, sealing wax secures the strings to the package. These are not neat boxes wrapped with crisp edges and thin wrapping paper. The paper appears to be a heavier stock and not decorative in nature. When creating your packages, start out with square stock of various sizes. All four sides have to be sanded smooth. If you round over the corners, that is not a problem. In fact slightly rounding over the corners is a good thing.

Sand all four sides with the grain, finishing up with 120 grit sand paper.

Cut the packages to size, using a fine tooth saw blade, then sand the end grain.

I'm using a 3/4" brad with the head cut off as my drill. Drill a small hole into one end of each package.

I insert a brad securely into the drill hole at what is now the bottom of the package. Once the brad is in place, put the packages in a small jig. The packages are now ready for texturing and painting. You need enough of the brad exposed beyond the end of the package to be securely held by needle nose pliers.

Burning & Painting Jultomten

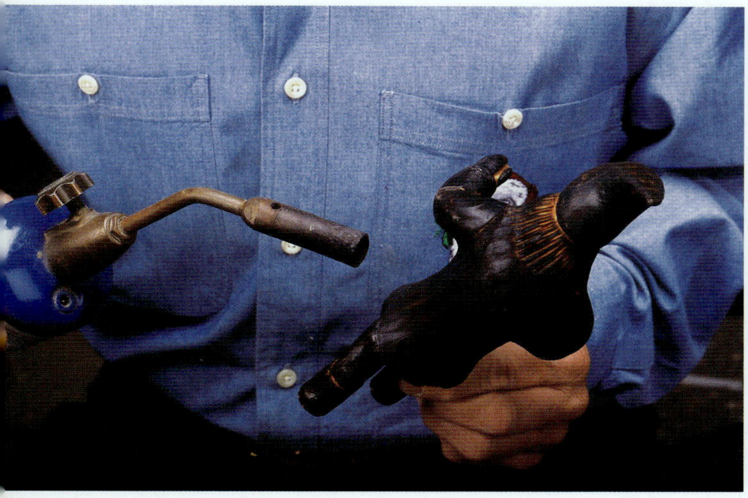

This particular step is not for the faint of heart. To soften the appearance of your carving, I use a burning torch. **Stop!** For photographic clarity, I'm neither using the torch in this image, nor wearing the proper protection, as I would be if actually working with this equipment. Be sure to wear a leather apron and leather glove during the actual burning procedure. Also , if you've used tupelo gum for the carving, you're going to have to be very, very careful. Tupelo burns very hot and fast. All other woods also need care when burning. Use the large torch for the back of the coat, hat, and other large areas. Keep away from the details with this torch.

Use the small detail torch for areas around the face, the tips of the boots, and especially the nose. When I burn, I always burn on the thicker parts and edges first. I hold the carving by the head and burn the fur, coat, and lower body first. My suggestion is to wear a leather glove on the hand that holds the carving and use a bare hand for the torch (which gives more control of the torch). Burn a little at a time. Do not let any of your wood glow or catch fire. Put any burning points on the leather apron and smother the flames against the apron front. When I switch the carving to burn the top, I usually use a small kitchen torch. It has a smaller flame and is easier to control. Try your best not to put the flame directly on the face. You should get enough peripheral burning to blacken the face without distorting the features.

Use a toothbrush to remove burned wood from the face and any other detail areas.

I use a kitchen scrubbing pad mounted on a flexible shaft tool to clean the rest of Jultomten. You need to clean with the grain. You may notice that your carving has checked, you may have uneven burning, you may have lost some detail, or you may find some "unusual" features in the wood you didn't know you had. I like to call all these things "patina." Leave them in place. It will make your carving your own. As I said, you are probably going to lose some detail during texturing. That is why we exaggerated the features earlier in the carving process. Depending on how much you lose, you may need to go back and touch up your carving.

There are several methods to seal your figure before painting. This is a semi gloss lacquer (sometimes I use sanding sealer) that can be either brushed on or sprayed.

The figure is now cleaned of burned wood.

The figure is coated with lacquer. You can build up your thickness by applying multiple coats of lacquer or sanding sealer.

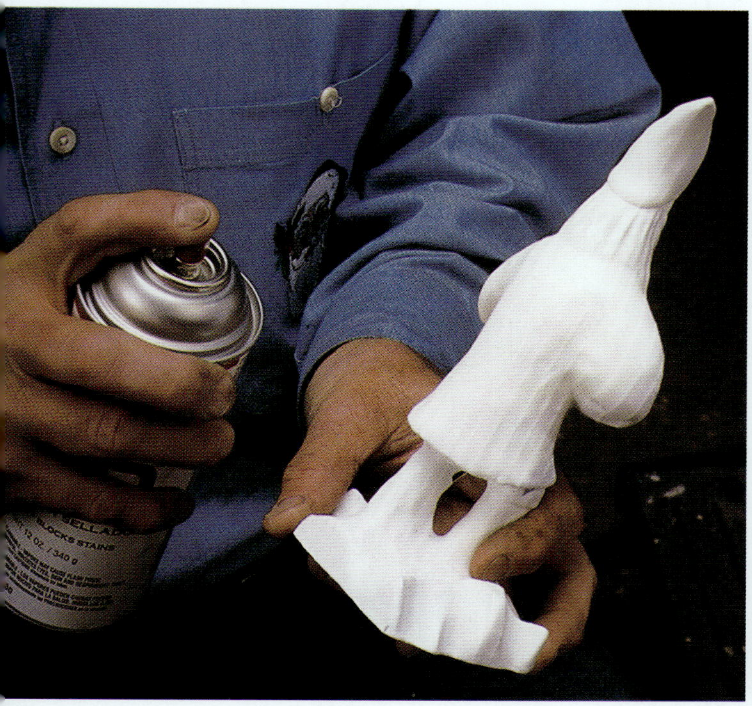

Another way to seal your carving is to use a quick dry oil-based white sealant. This sealer will also act as a primer. If you use spray primer, you will need to apply *multiple* coats to achieve the thick, even, smooth coating we desire.

You need to spend some time tapping the project with your finger, coaxing the excess sealer to run back down into the can. Don't attempt to apply sealer in this way unless you have the time to let it set up.

I came up with a *very unorthodox* method of applying white sealer to a figure. One day, while in a hurry, I dropped a piece in this sealer by mistake. Upon fishing it out, I found it had a thick, ceramic-like glaze that was smooth and uniform. This method does not prove to be any quicker, in fact the drying time is slower than drying times for brushed or sprayed on sealers. However, the end results, in my opinion, are far superior. Also, you can only do half of the figure at a time. It takes at least 12 solid hours in a heated room to dry.

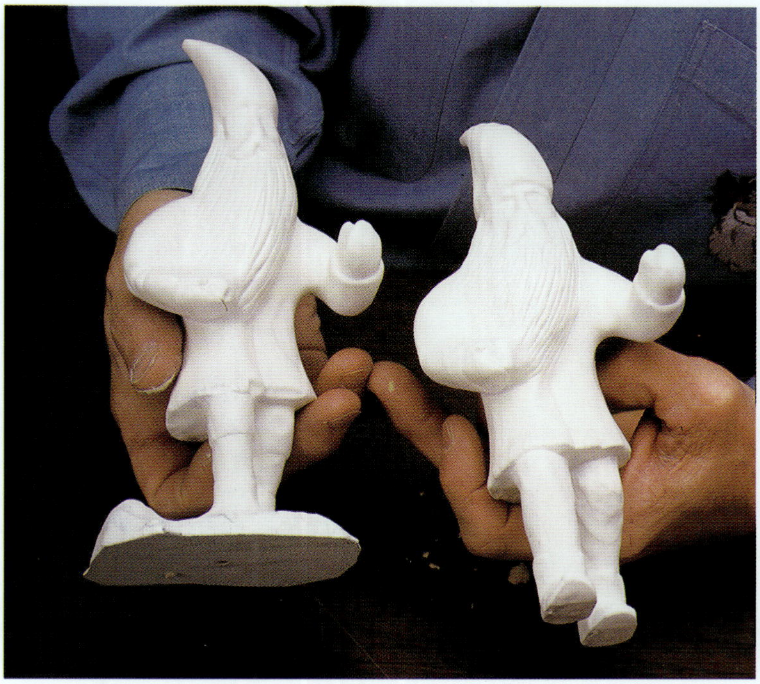

Sealer has been applied to both halves of the carving. You may need to take some fine sandpaper to smooth out any imperfections.

The rucksack has now been burned with the smaller torch. It has been cleaned and sealed with a semi gloss lacquer because I don't want a high sheen on this piece.

For the packages, I use a latex primer for two reasons: it comes out of the can thicker and, since I do all my detail painting in my paint room in the house, the latex primer has no odor. Dip the packages in the latex sealer just as you did the figure. This sealing method accentuates the rounded look of the packages carried by the Jultomten.

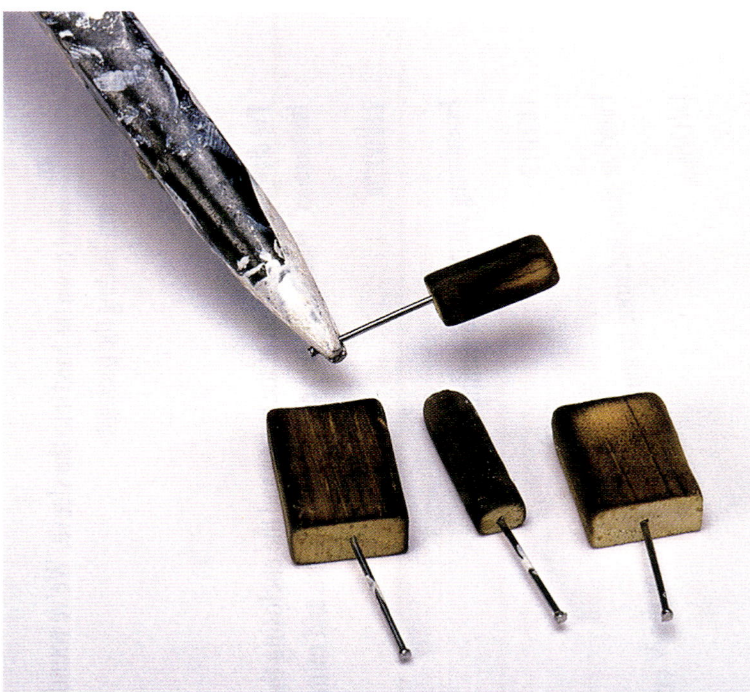

You may have wondered why we put the small brads in the bottoms of the packages. Use needle nose pliers to hold onto the brads while you burn the packages. The packages are burned, cleaned, and ready for painting.

The easiest place to let your packages dry is the small jig. Dip and place the packages using the needle nose pliers.

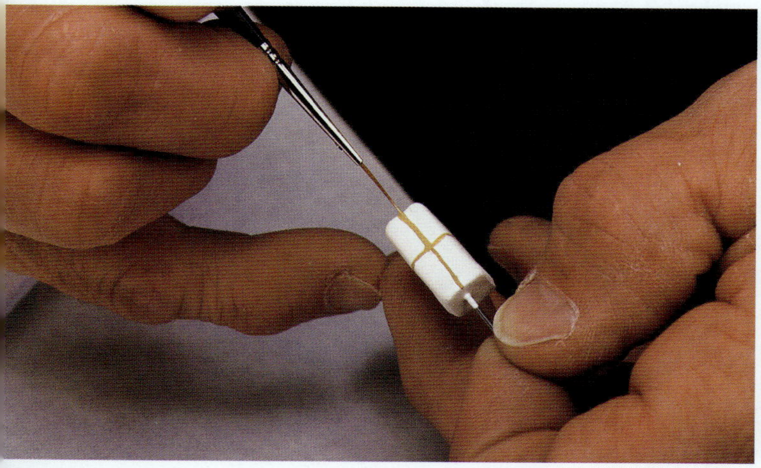

I use a liner brush and acrylic paints to hand paint the twine on the packages. In my research, most of the packages seem to be wrapped in a straw- or gold-colored twine.

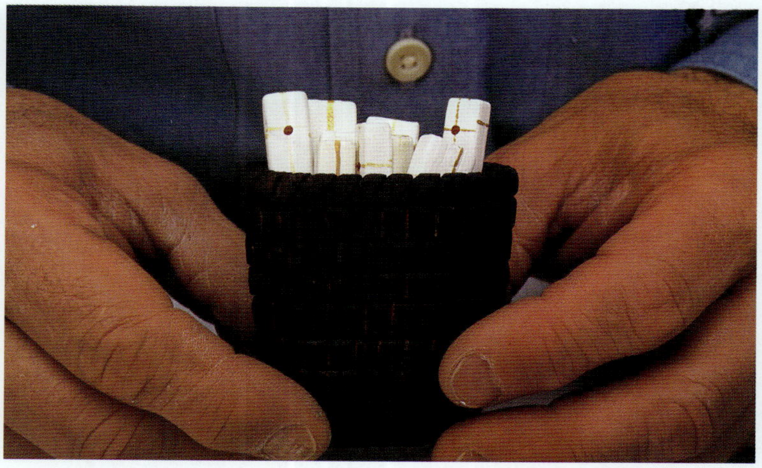

A rucksack full of presents, ready to be delivered to the homes of good children.

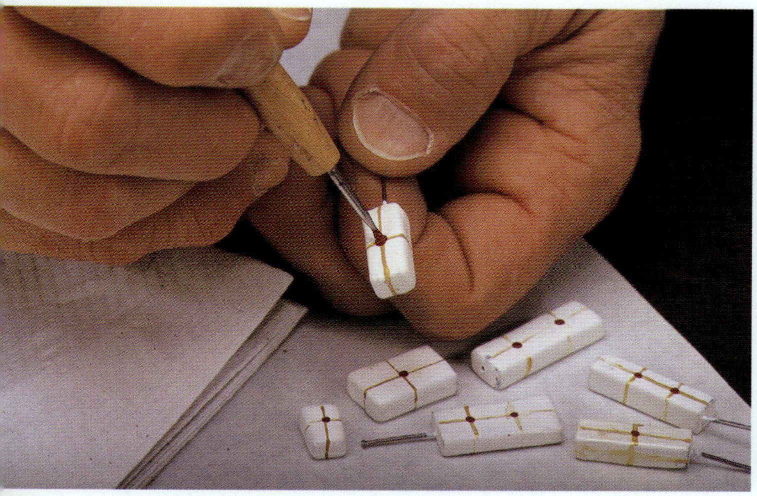

I use a stylus and thick acrylic gesso to create the effect of the sealing wax.

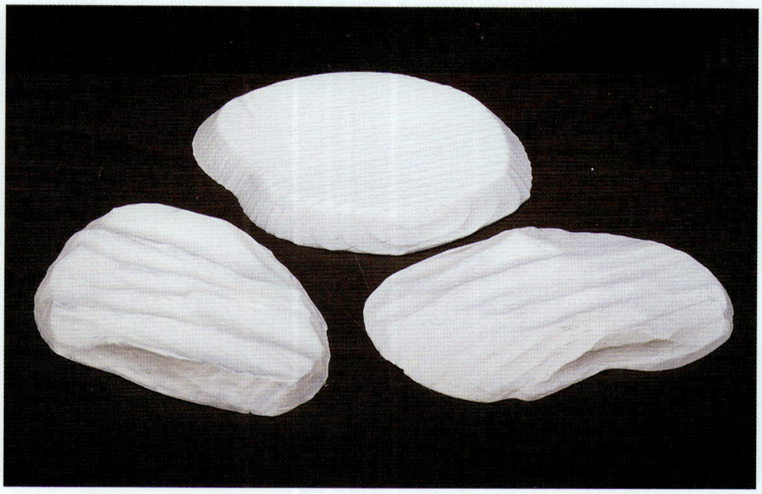

I have given you the options of two different textures on these three bases. The two bases in front are carved, burned, and sealed with white sealer. The base in the back has been burned very heavily, cleaned, and sealed. Since I wanted the grain to be more pronounced, I burned the back base heavily.

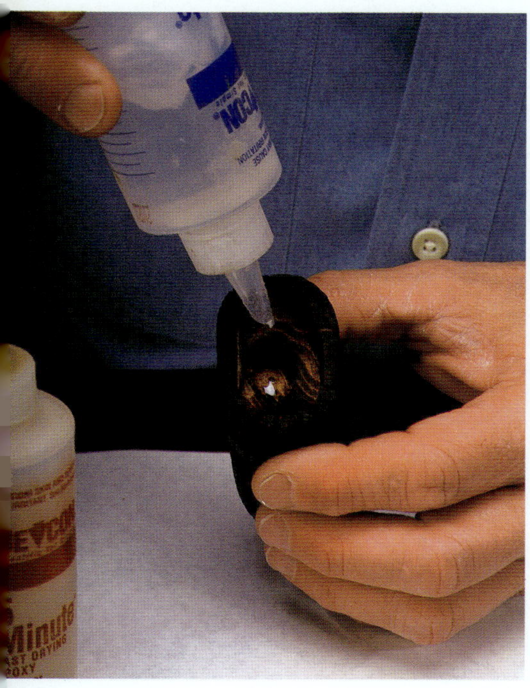

I mix up two part, five minute epoxy right inside the pack to fix the packages in place. Carefully place the packages in the pack, using varying sizes and shapes to create an interesting effect.

At this point, we're ready to place the tree and Jultomten on the base. Note that the tree has been burned and sealed. Since Jultomten is not quite dry yet, be very careful how you handle the figure.

Mark the approximate center of the tree and trace around Jultomten's feet.

Drill a 1/4" hole for the center of the tree and a pilot hole at the center of each heel.

Measure the width of the feet and use a Forstner bit of the same size to drill out flat spots for both feet in the base. If using a drill press, it is easy to set the press at the same depth for both feet. If you are hand drilling, you must try and try again until the feet are even on the base. If you decide to use a flat base, it is not necessary to drill for the feet.

Turn the base over and either countersink or counter bore a hole in the center of each pilot hole large enough to accommodate a screw head.

I coated the base with white spray primer, drilled a 1/4" hole in the base of the tree (carved and burned of course), and fit a length of 1/4" dowel rod in the hole.

I'm using hookers green to paint the evergreen tree. There are other greens available that work including pthalo green, sap green, and pine green.

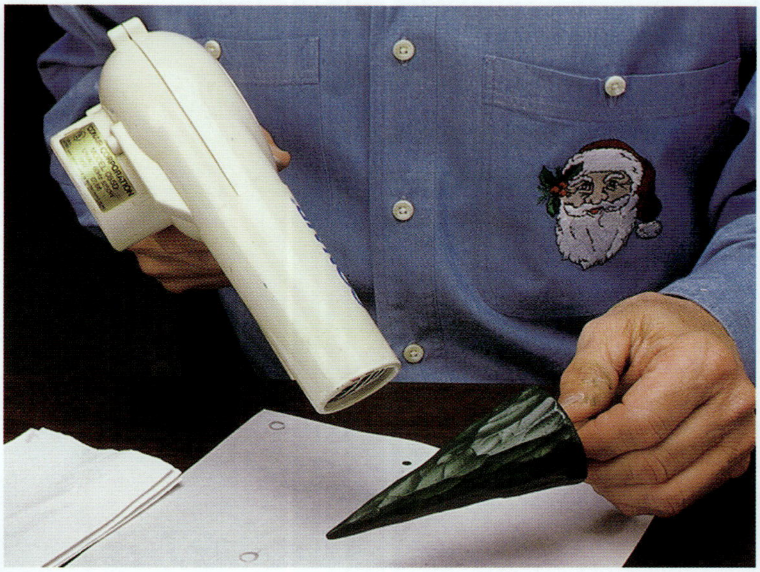

To speed the drying process with acrylic paints you can use a hair dryer. This technique does not work with any oil-based paints.

I'm using a dry sponge with white gesso, tapping lightly on the high spots on the tree, to apply snow.

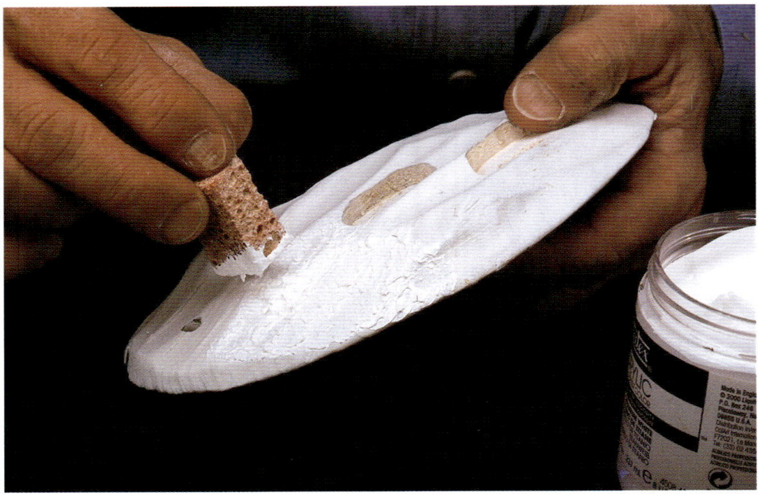

Set aside the tree to dry. Using a larger dry sponge and a high viscosity titanium white acrylic paint, most often referred to as "texture paint," dab the paint over the surface of the base to increase the snow effect.

Try to apply the texture paint a little heavily around the sharp lines cut in for the feet. Once Jultomten is in place, you may need to go back with the texture paint to blend in the base with the boots. The texture paint has been applied and the tree is fitted in place on the base.

The body and legs have been sprayed with the suede color. Working with this paint is always an adventure. For the first time ever, this paint crazed when applied. You can't be sure exactly what you'll get.

We've started to paint the figure, using suede texture paint. Once again, this is a rather unorthodox way of painting the carving, but I really like the texture this spray paint gives the finished product. This is just another way of painting, something a bit out of the ordinary but it works. Of course, feel free to use traditional paints on your carving if you wish. When using the spray paint, I find it handy to use a blocker to mask areas I wish to keep free of the color in use. This is a very low-tech way to mask these areas. Some spray paint is sure to get through.

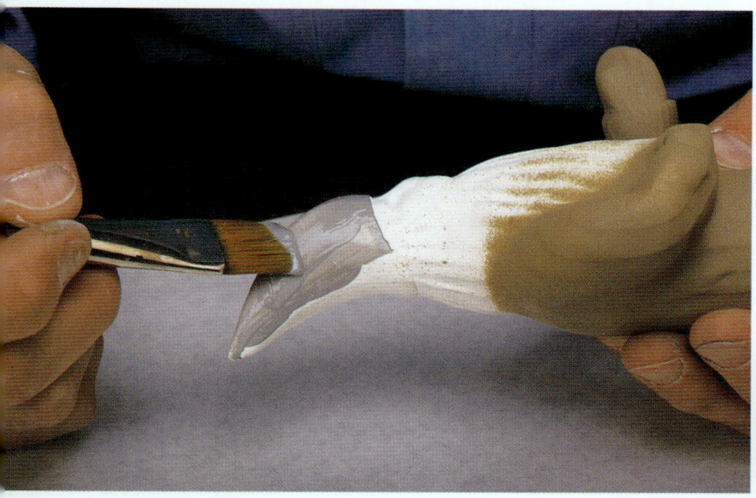

Use a first coat of gray gesso over a lightly sanded hat, the face, beard, mittens, and package.

Paint the hat and mittens red. I have found that the red paint works much better when it overlays the gray, rather than the white undercoat.

Like so.

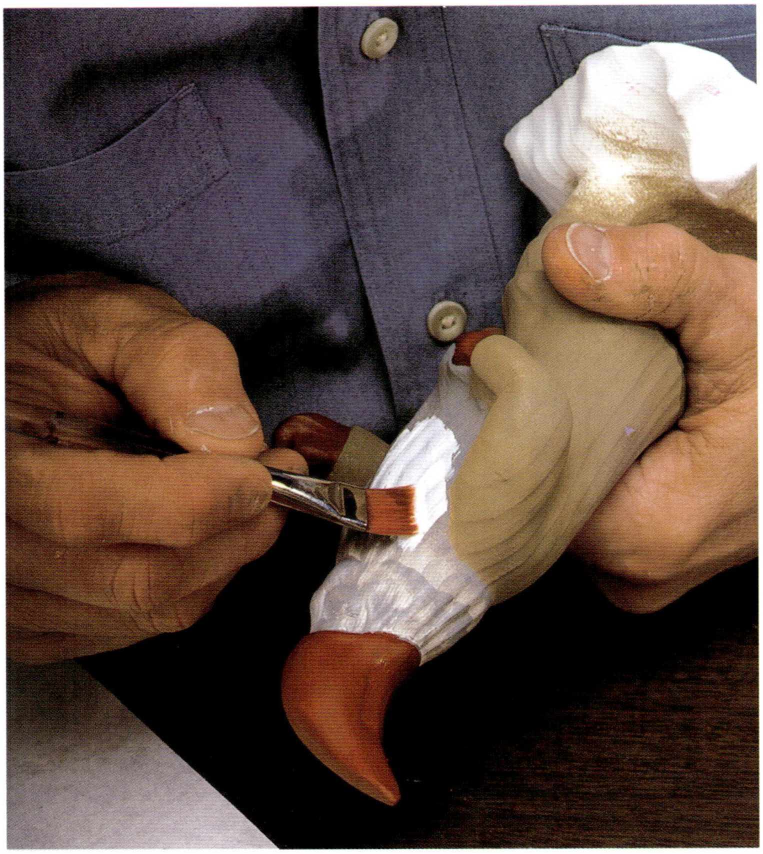

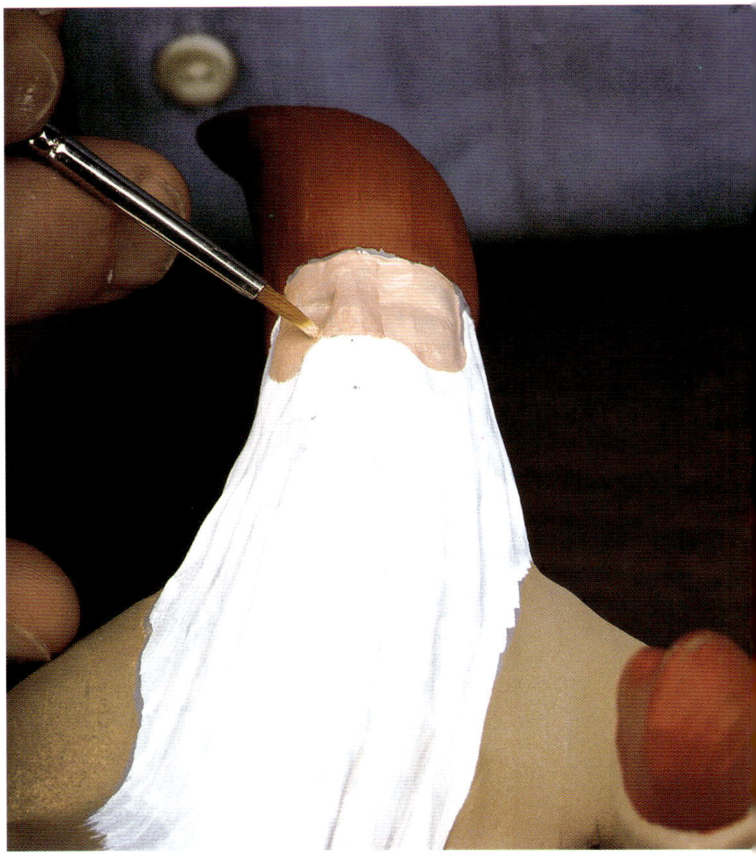

Paint the face flesh tone. Using burnt sienna and white makes a good flesh tone color.

Use white gesso to go back over the beard, hair, and package.

Apply a second coat of the flesh tone to the face. Mix titanium white with gesso and apply as a second coat to the beard and package.

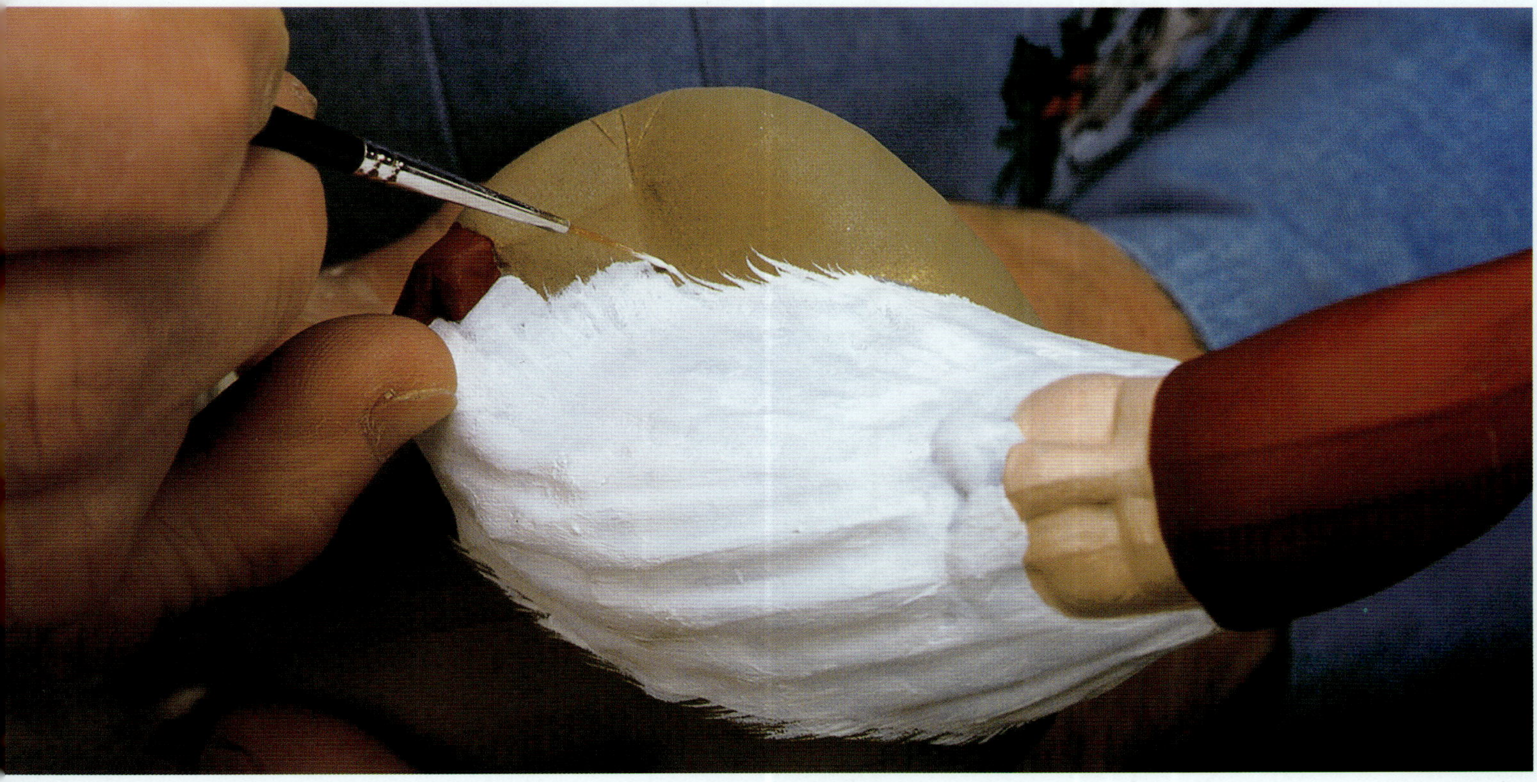

Using a liner brush, feather some of the titanium white and gesso out on the coat around the beard to create the impression of hair and avoid crisp, straight beard edges.

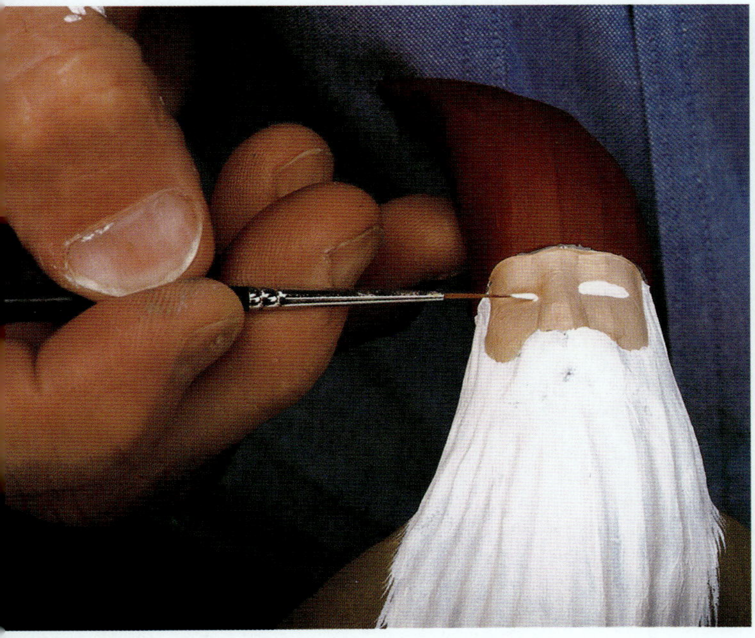

Using mostly titanium white, lay in the eye using a slight curve at the top and a flat line across the base of the eye. The eye tapers at the end.

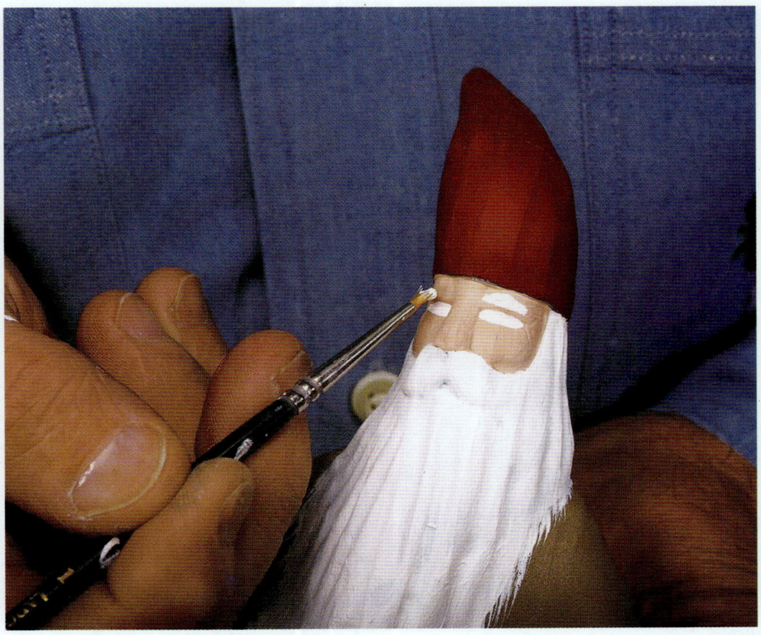

Use an old, small, stiff brush (I cut this brush down a bit) and texture paint to dab on the eyebrows.

The eyebrows are in place.

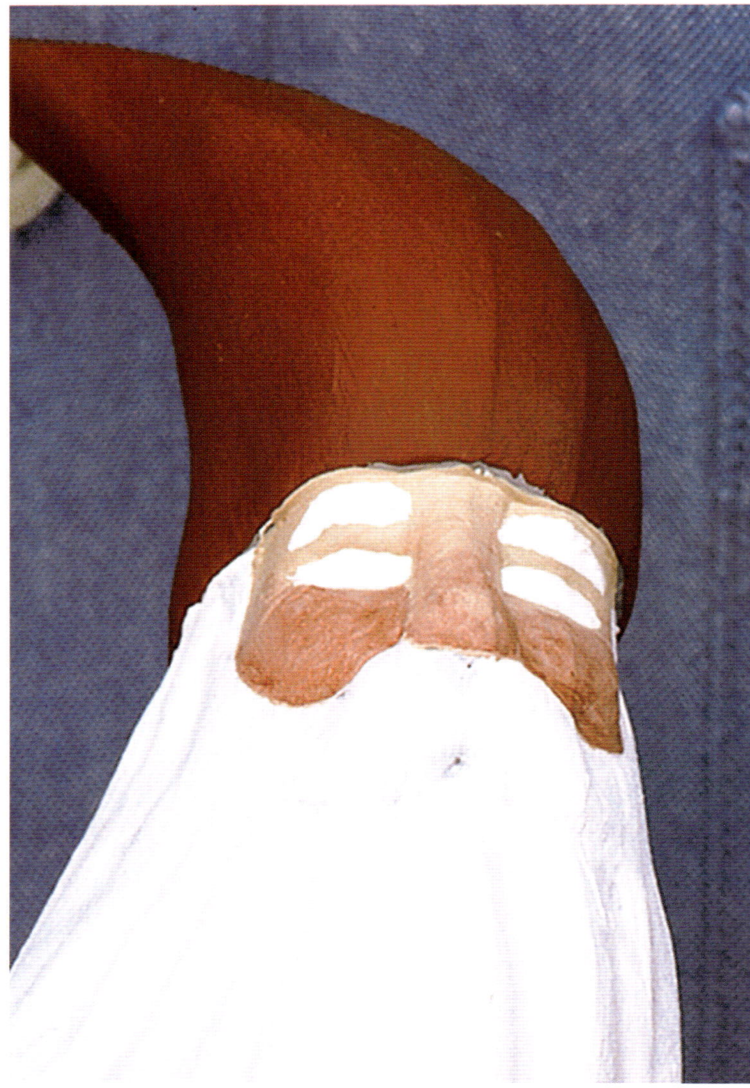

The rosy cheeks and nose have been added.

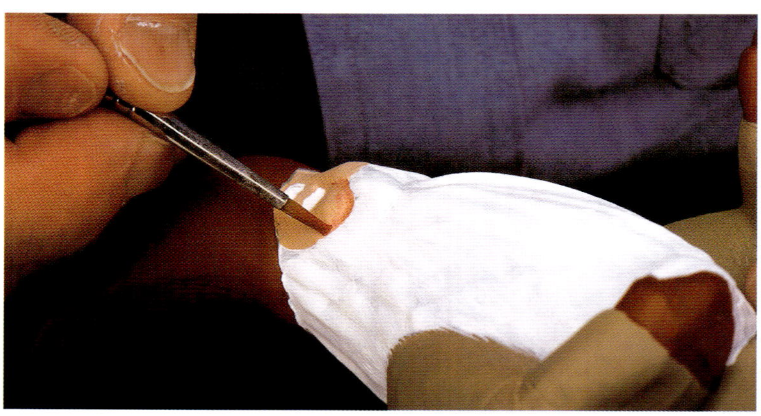

Add a very light wash of red at the base of the cheek along the beard line. Blend the red into the face to give the illusion of rosy cheeks in cold weather.

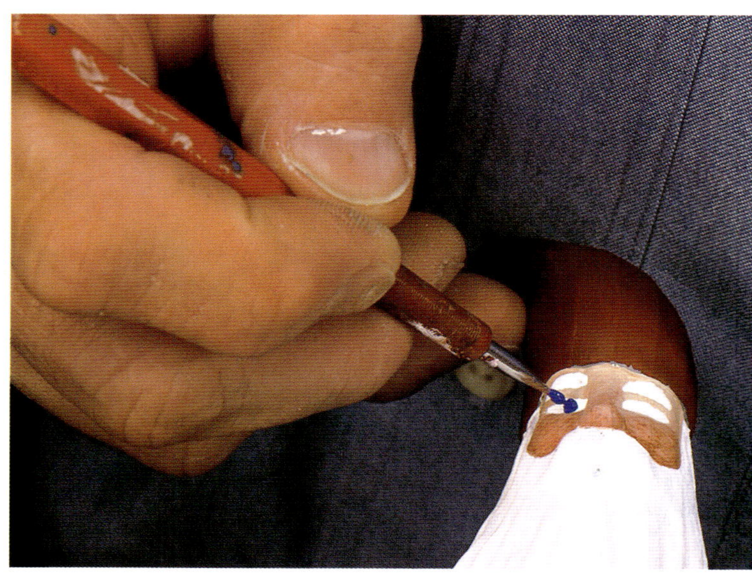

Add blue eyes using the stylus. I'm using Swedish blue paint. It is a mixture of ultra marine blue and phthalocyanine blue.

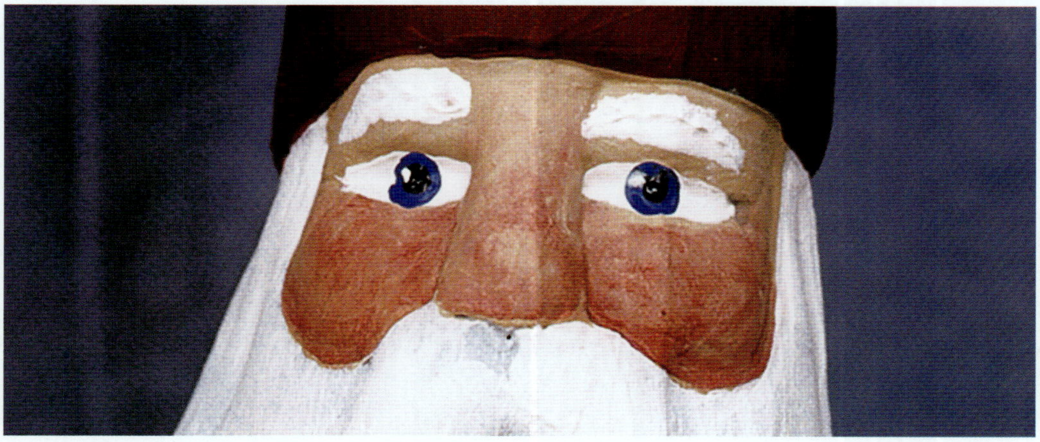

Add a black dot to the pupil and a white dot for the highlight. The highlight usually goes in the upper corner of the eye (right or left is your preference).

I'm using a permanent marker (burnt sienna in color) to add eyelashes and crow's feet. I also add a slight line on each side of the nose. Also highlight the bottom of the eyebrow. You can add gloss medium on the eye area only to give the eye a little more sheen.

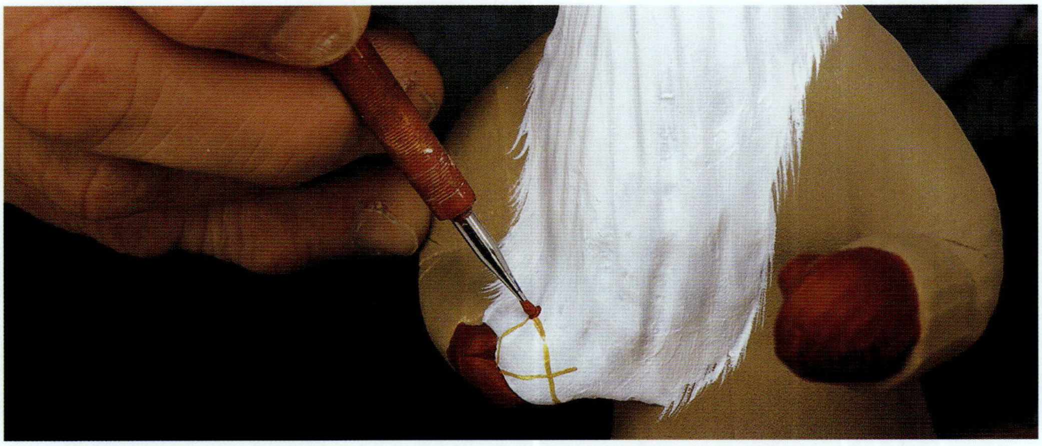

Take the liner brush and, using straw-colored (a mix of raw sienna and white) paint for gold, add the twine to the package in his right hand. Use permanent alizarin crimson hue for the sealing wax, which is applied to the intersections of the twine.

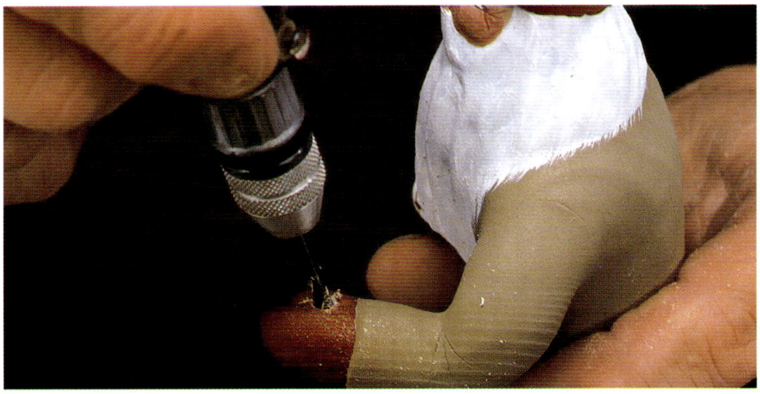

After your paint is thoroughly dry, drill a small pilot hole followed by a 1/8" drill hole through the mitten to hold the walking stick. Watch your angle. You want the stick to be well oriented to the body. The angle you choose for the hole will determine the angle of the walking stick.

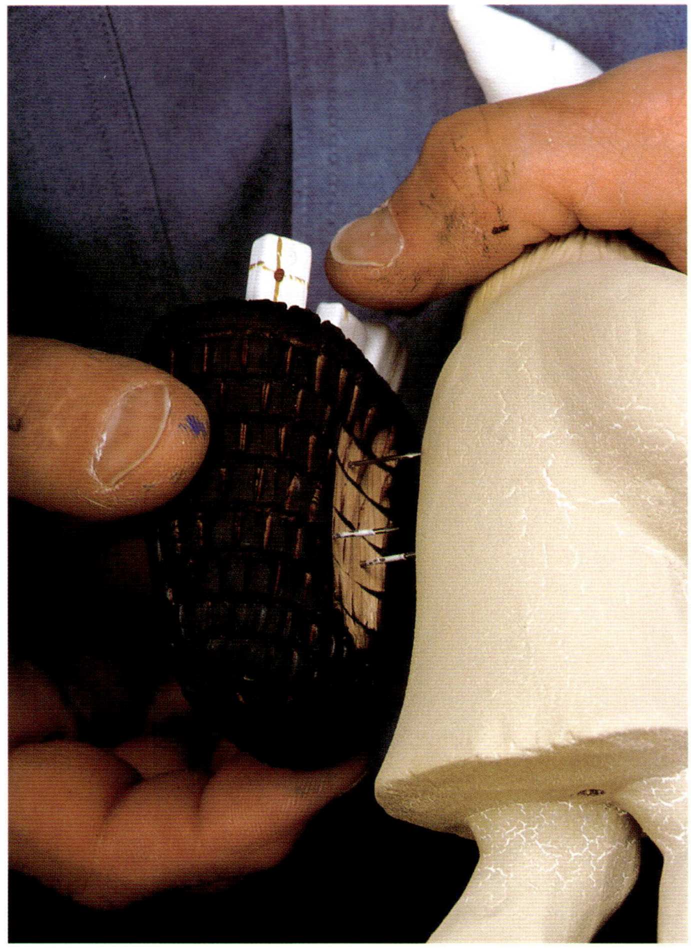

To attach the backpack, use three 3/4" inch brads set in the back of the backpack in a slight depression carved out to fit Jultomten's back. The depression gives more surface area for glue. The brads (placed into small drill holes) are for added security. Mix up five-minute epoxy for the rucksack. After drilling three matching holes in the back, I hold the rucksack to the back and make it secure. Make sure your figure is completely dry before applying this backpack.

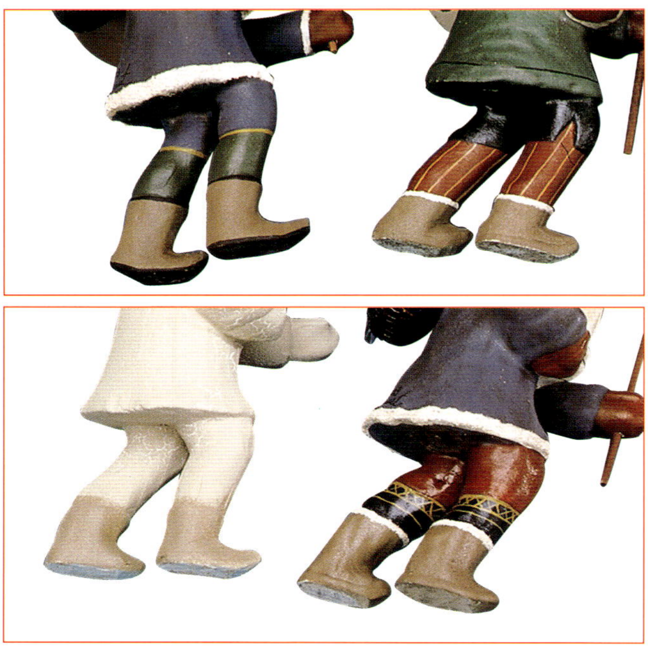

Now that the top half of the figure is finished and the pants are painted, it is time to concentrate on the boots. Our original, second from the right, shows boots with a slight over spray of buckskin paint. In fact all of the boots are buckskin with a little different trim. However, the final color choice for your boots is entirely up to you, from red to black, buckskin to brown. Note the different treatment of the boots, socks, and pants.

Add the walking stick, after the majority of the shaft has been tapered down to 1/8" diameter with a fairly blunt tapered bottom end and a larger top. The amount of stick you leave above the hand to finish the top of the walking stick is up to you. If the walking stick does not reach the base, this implies motion, with Jultomten in mid-stride and his stick in the air.

Stick in hand (without any glue) and the figure secured to the base, Jultomten is complete. Remember to use at least one dry wall screw through the bottom, up into the leg to secure the figure to the base. The base and tree have also been sprayed with a silver glitter to highlight the snow, creating the illusion of the sun glittering off the new fallen snow.

This picture shows two different carvings: the one on the left with Minwax™ Early American oil-based stain applied for antiquing. The other figure is stain free. The oil-based stain softens the colors, adds a patina to the figure, and provides a protective coating over the paint beneath. Apply the stain without the walking stick. Allow your paint at least a couple of days drying time before you apply any stain to your carving. Use a soft bristle brush to apply stain over the entire project. Use a clean, dry cloth to blot excess stain. Then use a large, clean, dry brush to remove excess stain. Use the cloth to keep the brush dry.

Gallery